I0789776

THE LOUD QUIET

LOVE, LAUGHTER, AND LIFE IN THE EMPTY NEST

RICK AND CLANCY DENTON

Copyright © 2026 by EX4CX LLC

All rights reserved. No part of this book may be reproduced in
any form without written permission from the publisher
or author, except as permitted by U.S. copyright law.

This book is for educational purposes only and does not
provide professional advice. The authors and publisher
disclaim any liability for errors, omissions, or outcomes related
to the use of the information contained herein.
Views expressed are solely those of the individuals involved
and do not represent any agency or organization.

Library of Congress Control Number: 2026904044

ISBN: 978-1-969267-06-2 (paperback)
ISBN: 978-1-969267-07-9 (ebook)

Published by Twin Flames Studios

"*The Loud Quiet* is a must-read for anyone navigating the empty-nest stage and adjusting to a new chapter of life. Clancy and Rick Denton have hit a home run. Their personal and poignant take on this universal midlife experience had me nodding yes to everything they shared. Their reflections on love, identity, and rediscovery deeply resonated with me. The title itself, *The Loud Quiet*, perfectly captures what happens when a home once filled with energy and noise suddenly becomes still. The Dentons explore that 'what now?' moment with honesty, humor, and heart."

—Tammy J Cohen,
Author of *Text Messages to My Sons*

"*The Loud Quiet* podcast got me through my first months as an empty nester, and it continues to inspire me today. Rick and Clancy have brought their highly practical guidance and fantastic personalities together to create a heartwarming, life-affirming book for those seeking to thrive in this dynamic season. This honest, candid, funny, totally human, and incredibly valuable book is a must-read for those wanting to enjoy life and flourish after raising kids. It's a much-needed masterpiece to help you navigate your empty nest journey!"

—Courtney Lynch, Attorney, CEO, and
Author of the *New York Times* bestseller *Spark*

"Watching Rick and Clancy grow *The Loud Quiet* from a podcast experiment into this beautiful book has been such a privilege. They've turned real conversations about marriage, identity, and rediscovery into something that feels both deeply personal and universally relatable. From the bittersweet tears of move-in day to the humor of realizing you can eat dinner at 5:30 just because you can, their storytelling captures it all. *The Loud Quiet* reminds us that this season of life isn't empty at all; it's wide open."

—Marc Ronick,
Podcast Producer and Coach at iRonick Media

"The empty nest can feel like such a strange and transformative phase in life, and this book offers an incredibly honest and relatable look at one family's journey through it. It dives deep into the challenges parents face as their grown children leave home, navigating shifts in family dynamics, rediscovering their relationship as a couple, and adjusting to a new chapter in their lives. It's a truly authentic, heartfelt exploration of a pivotal time in life."

—JP and Aeryn Shiffer, Frequent Guests on
The Loud Quiet - Empty Nest Living Podcast

To our children, Tanner and Teagan,

Our reasons for this book.

*You've left our nest, and we love
watching you thrive in life.*

Table of Contents

Part I: Fall

Part IV: Summer

Author's Note

We wrote this book in 2025, but the stories inside it began in 2023. Back then, we hit record on a little podcast experiment called *The Loud Quiet,* thinking it would be a way to process our first year as empty nesters. What we didn't realize was that those conversations, sometimes funny, sometimes tender, sometimes awkward, would become the backbone of this book.

So here's where we stand now. By the time these words reach you, Tanner is in law school, and Teagan is nearing the end of her undergrad years. Clancy has retired from one career and stepped into something new. Rick exited the consulting world and has gone 100 percent into the podcasting business together with Clancy. And together is really the point. We're in this season as partners, figuring it out in real time.

This book isn't a manual. It's not a three-step program. It's a snapshot, a collection of conversations, memories, and reflections from the messy, beautiful, sometimes hilarious in-between. We hope you'll find pieces of your story here. And maybe, as you read, you'll feel like you've pulled up a chair at our table, poured yourself a glass of whatever fits the hour, and joined the conversation.

Foreword

by Tanner and Teagan Denton

Our parents have taken on many roles through-out their lives. Flight attendant, consultant, fitness instructor, podcaster, to name a few. "Published book author" was not a role we ever would have anticipated our parents to take on! And we are so excited that they are sharing this dream with the world.

Growing up, our parents gave us everything we needed to find our paths. They cheered at games, stayed up for late-night talks, and endured the chaos of teenage years. What we didn't realize then was that, in preparing us to go, they were also preparing themselves to let go.

Watching them now, as empty nesters, is some-times still a bit strange. Sure, there were a few quiet dinners and "we miss you" texts at first, but before long, they were discovering what life would look like when it was just the two of them again. It's been amazing to see them undertake all sorts of new experiences and hobbies together.

Mom and Dad, we're so proud of you. You've shown us that life keeps unfolding, that change can be beautiful, and that the bonds we built will always hold. The nest might be empty, but the love that built it never leaves.

Family vacation to Iceland

A Beginning, Sort Of

It was spring, just before our daughter's high school graduation. Our son was already off at college, and we were deep in the rituals of her senior year: awards nights, final performances, late-night group texts about party invitations, and cap-and-gown pickups. The kind of busy that feels suspended in nostalgia, half in the moment, half already missing it.

One night, we went out for dinner, just the two of us. We ordered martinis, made small talk about the week ahead, and joked about the end of an era.

And then, somewhere between the second round and the trip home, Clancy turned to Rick and said, "What if I don't like *us* when she leaves?"

The silence was immediate and deafening.

Rick: By the time we pulled into the driveway, I had that sick-in-your-stomach, head-in-your-hands kind of feeling. I sat on the edge of the bathtub while Clancy got ready for bed, trying to make sense of the panic curling in my chest. I've lost things before: my dad, who passed when I was a young adult, jobs, and a sense of certainty. But our marriage had always been the constant. And suddenly, it felt like even that was up for grabs.

Clancy: I wasn't trying to start a crisis. I was trying to tell the truth, that I was scared. That fear had been circling for months before I found the words to express it.

Asking the question cracked something open. Eventually, by naming it, we turned "what if" into "how can we…"

How can we stay connected without the kids?

How can we rediscover who we are, not just as parents but as partners?

How can we remember that we don't just love each other but still *like* being together, too?

• • •

We didn't set out to make a podcast or write a book. This whole thing started as a way for us to reconnect as a couple. To talk about the weirdness, the quiet, the sudden abundance of time. About the grief that sneaks up between the granola bars and the cereal aisle.

We didn't have any answers, but we knew that by asking the questions, we'd at the very least find something interesting to talk about.

What happens when the school drop-offs stop?

When the Friday night football games are no longer on the calendar, but your brain still saves space for them?

When your social life has been built around sideline chats and concession stand hot dogs, and suddenly, it's Friday, and there's nothing scheduled?

That's where we were.

And maybe where you are, too.

So much of our life—our routines, our conversations, even our friendships—had been orbiting around the kids. And now, the center of gravity had shifted. We were still spinning, but in a different sky.

We weren't the only ones. That's part of what sparked this whole thing. We have friends ahead of us in the empty nest phase. Friends behind us. Friends in the checkout line at Target, deciding which brand of twin XL sheets makes it easier to say goodbye. And all of us are asking some version of the same thing:

Who are we now?

Who are *we* when it's just Tuesday night and there's no homework, no drill team, no curfew?

Who am *I* when the kids I've poured myself into are out there living lives of their own?

Let's be clear: this isn't a "poor us" story. We're thrilled for them. Seriously. Seeing their excitement, their growth... it's what we hoped for. But it's also weird. Because the house *is* quieter, and sometimes that quiet feels so loud, it echoes.

Hence the name: *The Loud Quiet.*

It's that ache when you pass their empty bedroom.

The strange elation of realizing you don't have to plan dinner around anyone else's schedule.

The laugh you share with your partner about finally finding a happy hour spot and then realizing you don't have to rush home.

It's messy. It's beautiful. It's deeply human.

And we wanted to talk about it.

Not from a stage. Not from a place of expertise. Just from a couple of chairs, with the cat occasionally wandering by, and the mic between us. A little podcast that turned into this book.

So if you're here, you might be somewhere on the same road.

Maybe your house just got quieter.

Maybe you're staring down the countdown calendar to college move-in.

Maybe you've already repainted the bedroom and replaced the posters with tasteful throw pillows. (Or maybe not. No judgment either way.)

Wherever you are, we're glad you're here.

This book is our conversation. Sometimes it's Rick reflecting on old memories. Sometimes it's Clancy with a practical insight or a heart-on-her-sleeve moment. Sometimes it's both of us, arguing gently over dinner plans and processing this next chapter together.

We're not here to give you a step-by-step plan. We don't have one.

We're figuring it out, too.

But what we *can* offer is a hand to hold, a story to share, a laugh when you need it, and a tissue when you don't know why you're crying in the parking lot of At Home.

We started this whole thing with a lot of questions. And honestly, we still have them.

But if there's one thing we *do* know, it's this:

Empty nest is a terrible name. Because this life stage is the opposite of empty. It is full of memory and meaning. Full of space for rediscovery, for reconnection. For late-night takeout and mid-morning walks. For grief and joy and awkward transitions and unexpected laughter.

It's not the absence of something.

It's the beginning of something else.

PART I

Fall

1

Ramen, Rugs, and Reality

We joked that we were just on a weekend trip. Two small carry-ons. Some snacks. A few too many Target runs.

It didn't feel like a final chapter... not at first.

We had done this once before with Tanner, so we told ourselves this would be easier. Familiar, even. We knew the drill: Pack up the IKEA bags (big blue miracles of modern engineering), fly to Arizona, help her settle in, grab a margarita somewhere, and try not to cry at the airport. That was the plan.

And yet, somewhere between Walmart #3 and the plastic horse in her car, it started to unravel.

• • •

It's funny, the things that tip you over.

For Clancy, it was a packet of ramen left in the pantry—forgotten, crinkled, and somehow devastating. For Rick, it was the sight of little plastic animals tumbling around the floor of Teagan's car. "The horse fell off," he said, half-laughing, half-swallowing something bigger.

We both knew it then: The emotions weren't waiting for the big goodbye. They were already here, hiding in the crumbs and corners.

• • •

The whole weekend felt like one long moving sidewalk, one of those airport ones where you can't quite get off. Every step pulled us closer to *the moment*.

Check into hotel.

Find a burger place.

Hit three Targets and four Walmarts.

Shop for rugs (always the rugs).

Meet the roommate. Smile for pictures. Try not to think about the Last Night.

We stayed busy on purpose. Busy makes it easier. Busy gives your brain something to do besides scream, *This is happening*. Busy meant we could still pretend it was just a trip.

But in the quiet moments, the drive to the dorm, the silence in the car while she rode with her brother, the sad 80s song on the radio, we could feel it creeping in.

• • •

Move-in day was chaos.

Not emotional chaos. Literal, logistical chaos. We had 30 minutes to unload before the parking gods issued a ticket, so it was a sprint. (Note to future empty nesters: Bring a bin, set an alarm, and make peace with forgetting at least one extension cord.)

Tanner was a hero that day, helping us carry boxes and keep pace. Thank God he was there. Not just for the muscles but for the energy. For the presence.

There was an explosion of stuff in the hallway. Not literal. (Rick insists we clarify.) But rugs and shelves and plastic drawers and whatever mystical combination of twinkle lights and succulents count as "dorm cozy" now.

We didn't stop. Not really. Not until she turned around, tears silently falling, and said, "I miss my cat."

Not us.

The cat.

We cried anyway.

• • •

That night, we dropped her off and watched her walk up to her dorm. Just as we were pulling away, we saw her pause and help another girl figure out the door code.

They walked in together.

And that—that was the moment.

It wasn't a speech. It wasn't a hug. It wasn't even from her to us. But it was what we needed: the tiniest spark of her making her own way.

A moment of grace. Of *okayness*.

• • •

The next day, we were invited to what was labeled a "parent information session." We almost skipped it. We'd been to enough orientations and info dumps over the years to fill a binder.

But we stayed. And when they handed us envelopes and blank paper, we realized that this wasn't paperwork.

It was a letter.

To her.

To be delivered at the end of her freshman welcome week.

Cue the tears.

Rick cried openly at the table. (Four other dads hid in the bathroom.) Clancy had already written one and snuck it into Teagan's suitcase, of course. But this felt different: raw, immediate, still vibrating from the day before.

Trying to put into words the whole messy, magical, heart-bursting truth of parenting in a few paragraphs was impossible. But we tried.

Because that's what this whole phase is: trying. Letting go. Crying. Writing. Praying. Hoping.

Buying the right surge protector. And walking away from your child down a dorm hallway, heart in your throat, wondering if they'll be okay.

And then seeing that they already are.

• • •

Later that night, we drove to see Tanner.

The buffer we didn't know we needed.

He's a senior now. Thriving. Making his own Target lists. (Okay, we still pay. Some things never change.) But watching him, we remembered that this transition isn't the end.

It's the beginning of something else.

Something beautiful. Weird. Quiet. And loud.

• • •

On the flight home, Clancy cried over a mushy good-bye text. Rick ordered one last lounge drink and sent a group message that turned into a collective puddle of feelings.

Then Tanner texted: "Hey, can I get your Gmail password for YouTube TV?"

Reality. Restored.

• • •

When we got home, the house was too quiet. Even the cat was confused.

But there was something else underneath the silence.

Space.

Not empty space—*open* space.

And maybe, just maybe, that's where the next version of us begins.

2

Routine(ish)

We thought we'd crave the quiet, or at least appreciate it. We'd talked about it enough, how nice it would be to just come home, sit down, not have to coordinate three dinner schedules and a carpool. But when it actually showed up, the silence didn't whisper. It thudded.

That first week post-drop-off, we tried to slide back into normal. Rick went to the gym. Clancy went to the grocery store. Only this time, the grocery cart looked like it belonged to a sad single person who lives on Greek yogurt and denial. One bag. No bulk snacks. No five-pack of chicken thighs. Just enough food for two adults who suddenly realized they had no idea how much they'd been eating in solidarity with a college kid.

The house started playing tricks on us. The trash can felt suspiciously light, like, wait, did something break? Is it trash day? Are we just... clean now? Then there was that same weird silence that makes you second-guess whether the dishwasher ran or if your hearing is just going.

We kept bumping into ghosts of our routines. The first day of school pictures still happened. Tanner and Teagan, sweet as they are, sent them in from their campuses. (Clancy may have cried. Rick may have pretended not to notice.) There was no one standing by the front door, but the tradition lived on. Sort of. Routine-ish.

And that became the theme of our week. We still woke up early. Still went to the gym. Still made it to work. But there was something off kilter. Like someone had picked up our house, given it a little shake, and then set it back down slightly askew. Things were familiar but different. Normal but eerie.

Even little things, like walking past the table and only setting two places. Or realizing we could eat whenever we wanted. (The AARP early bird special has never looked so good. We're not saying we've given in, but we've noticed the 5:30 dinner crowd is surprisingly chill.)

We started getting texts. "Where's my rain jacket?" "Did I bring my jewelry box?" It was like being haunted by logistical poltergeists. But we loved it. Because it meant they still needed us. A little. Enough.

By Saturday, we were crawling out of our skins. The weekend calendar was blank for the first time in forever. So we did what any two rational grown-ups rediscovering freedom would do: We drove to Fort Worth.

The Kimbell Art Museum gave us air conditioning and culture, both top-tier empty-nest coping mechanisms. We wandered through the galleries, argued gently over which paintings were the creepiest, and remembered what it's like to just be in each other's company, not in transit, not in task-mode. Just together.

We had a cocktail at a speakeasy that used to be a bookstore (of course), and Clancy ordered a Kir Royale. When the bartender didn't know what that was, she explained it. Champagne and cassis. Simple. Delicious. The bartender tasted it, smiled, and named it "The Clancy."

There's something about that. Reclaiming a name. Reclaiming a rhythm. Reclaiming a Saturday.

The next day, we hit a wall. Sunday came, and with it, the loud quiet. The kids were gone. The chores were done. There was no game to drive to. No load of laundry to fold. Just... nothing. Clancy said it first, "I'm bored." Like her soul didn't know where to sit.

That silence was so thick it became a presence. Rick tried to read a magazine. Clancy paced. We were both waiting for the house to return to its regularly scheduled programming. But this is the new show now. And it doesn't have a laugh track.

We'll figure it out. We're already starting to. With two placemats. With impromptu art dates, early dinners, and FaceTimes that make the cat meow. With reminders that being needed doesn't always mean being near. And with the knowledge that, for better or weirder, this new routine is ours.

3

The Gift in the Crappy Box

You think you know what empty nesting will look like.

We thought we did, anyway.

We pictured the quiet. The clean kitchen. The unstacked laundry baskets. Maybe some travel. More date nights. Fewer football games. That sense of freedom that sneaks in after years of juggling kids, calendars, and carpools.

But here's the plot twist nobody tells you about: Sometimes, when your kids leave, your parents need you more than ever.

And just like that, the roles reverse.

Rick

My mom used to be one of the brightest people in any room. Truly. Sharp as hell. A nurse turned office manager back when medical practices were independent beasts. She basically kept my dad's entire operation running without ever needing the title. She got her MBA from the University of Texas when I was in high school. And I don't mean that symbolically. I mean, we graduated at the same time. I had more hair then. She probably did, too.

She became a travel agent later in life, but not in the "package deal to Cancun" sense. She planned international adventures: India, China, and Germany in December for the Christmas markets (where Clancy was technically pregnant with Teagan, which means Teagan was there too, sort of). She took our son to England for a soccer pilgrimage: Chelsea FC at Stamford Bridge. She froze through a match with the diehard supporters, probably hating every minute, but beaming the whole time because she got to do it with her grandson.

That's who my mom was.

Clancy

And then, a few short years later, she wasn't.

Rick

She took a trip to Africa in 2019. When she got back, we got a phone call from one of the women she had traveled with, someone with healthcare experience. She told my sister, "I think something's wrong. I think you need to look into this."

At first, we brushed it off. My mom was busy. She forgot things because she was always juggling so much. Right?

But then we heard she had gotten disoriented at the Amsterdam airport. Couldn't find the restroom. Couldn't find her gate. This wasn't rural Mongolia; this was Schiphol. Well-lit. Well-signed. Something wasn't right.

In 2020, during the thick of COVID, we got the diagnosis: Alzheimer's.

Clancy

She was still conversational for a while. We'd do weekly Zoom calls. She'd ask about the kids, though she might forget who went to which college. But she was still herself, mostly. Still wanted to talk, to connect, to plan a future that didn't exist.

Rick

By 2022, we had to make the decision to move her into memory care.

And if you've ever had to do that, you know what kind of hell that is.

It was easier once we got her settled because she seemed to like it, so much so that she talked about buying property nearby so she and my dad could settle down there (never mind that he'd been gone for over a decade). In her mind, he was still very much a part of the plan. She told us she was thinking about schools for the grandkids, too. She thought Teagan might want to attend the one she was currently living in, the care facility, because it just seemed like such a lovely place.

It was sweet, and sad, and surreal. This version of reality she was living in was real to her. And in those moments, we just had to meet her there.

Clancy

It's not just the logistics; it's the heartbreak. It's the knowing that this fiercely independent, worldly, brilliant woman now needs help eating lunch.

But it was the right place. And we are incredibly thankful for the care team. For the aides who have developed deep, real relationships with her. For her husband, Jerry, who shows up twice a day, every day. He's our hero in all of this.

Rick

We don't live in Austin. So my role as caregiver looks different. I can't be there every day. I can't brush her hair or help her walk. But I can manage her rental home. I can make sure the bills get paid, the taxes get filed, and the little things stay afloat so Jerry doesn't have to carry it all.

I go down as often as I can. Clancy and I now take early-morning flights, do the visit, have a martini at Roaring Fork, and fly home that night. It's weird how those trips have become something we look forward to. Even in the sadness. Especially in the sadness.

Clancy

Because here's the thing: Empty nesting gave us the space to show up in this way.

We couldn't have done this a few years ago, not with cheer practice, carpool, and high school football games. But now? Now we can be there. We *get* to be there.

That's the gift in the crappy box.

The wrapping sucks. The box is beat up. But inside is this tiny, shimmering sliver of connection, of rediscovery. With each other. With your family. With the people you thought you'd always have time with.

Rick

I hate what this disease has done to my mom. Hate it. And sometimes, all I can do is laugh because the grief is so big it swallows everything. Like when we played our podcast for her and she yawned. A huge, slow-motion yawn. I think that was her soul's way of telling me, "Wrap it up, Rick. You're rambling again."

Clancy

And if we hadn't prepared? If we didn't have powers of attorney, legal documents, and bank accounts squared away?

Oh, it would've been a nightmare.

But we did. And now we're helping Nana (Rick's grandmother) do the same. We're trying to make the hard stuff a little less hard so we can focus on what matters most: being present, being kind, and loving the people in front of us, even when they don't remember who we are.

Rick

There's a line I jotted down somewhere; I wish I had it in front of me. But the gist is this: *Don't wait to access the wisdom of the generation before you. Because one day, that wisdom will be gone.*

We don't get to choose when the conversations end. But we do get to show up for them while they're still possible. And that, maybe more than anything, is what this season of life is asking us to do.

4

Do We Still Like Each Other?

We were catching up with friends the other night, a couple we adore, and they shared something that's been echoing in our heads ever since.

It was right after they dropped their only child off at college. They'd done all the prep: the dorm shopping, the Target runs, the graduation chaos, and the packing. The whole conveyor belt of parenting a kid out the door. But after the goodbye hug (the kind that hits you in the chest five seconds after it's over), they got in the car, sat in silence, and then she started crying.

Not just a tear or two. Full-on, "ugly cry" meltdown, as she put it.

And somewhere between mile 3 and mile 30 of that drive home, she asked the question, "What if we don't even like each other anymore?"

That landed hard. Because yeah, we've asked that question, too.

And that's the moment no one really wants to talk about.

Oh sure, people *warn* you about the empty nest. They say the house will feel quiet. That it'll hit you when you walk past their empty room or set one too many plates at dinner.

But what they don't say, or maybe what we just don't want to hear, is this: One day, you'll look across the table at the person you've spent decades raising children with and realize you're not entirely sure who they are without the kids in the room.

There's no manual for that. (And if there is, we didn't read it... which checks out.)

Our friends were brave enough to tell us what happened next.

They didn't have a slow ramp into the empty nest. Their son was an only child, which meant it wasn't a series of soft goodbyes. It was a cliff drop. One minute, everything revolved around their kid— the routines, the school calendars, the summer job schedules, the Taco Tuesdays—and the next minute, silence.

No practice run. No buffer sibling still under the roof. Just a hard stop and a long drive home.

Well, silence plus a minor identity crisis.

They did what a lot of us might do: They got busy. First came the redecorating. She tackled his bedroom with the energy of someone trying to exorcise a ghost. Furniture out. Walls repainted. Childhood posters pulled down like they'd started mocking her. It wasn't about erasing him; it was about trying to *anchor* herself in a room that suddenly felt like an ache.

They already had one dog. But after their son left, they got a second, so they "could each have one," they said with a laugh.

(And because emotional chaos loves company, we suppose.)

But even with the noise and the fur and the endless trips to Home Depot, the house still felt different. They still felt different. Because underneath all that motion, beneath the paint samples and vet appointments, was a quieter question starting to surface.

The one so many couples face but rarely say out loud: "What are we now if we're not parenting together?"

Here's the thing. Parenting is a beautiful and distracting kind of glue. You can stick with someone for years, decades, because there's always something urgent to do. A game to get to. A permission slip to sign. A meltdown to navigate. You can build a whole life in tandem without actually checking in to see how the *we* is doing.

And then one day, you're alone. The permission slips are gone. The lunchboxes are gone. You're not standing on the same sideline anymore. And you think, *Do we even like each other when we're not talking about the kid?*

Our friends didn't find answers overnight. But slowly, they started to move again.

He continued to play volleyball. She turned to books and Bravo to fill the quiet hours. And together, they signed up for something that felt both playful and slightly terrifying: dance lessons. Just the two of them, standing across from each other, trying to remember how to move in sync without stepping on each other's toes.

Which kind of felt like a metaphor for this whole phase of life.

We didn't talk much while they told us about it. We just listened. And thought about our story.

About how Rick started making solo grocery runs just to get out of the house. About how Clancy couldn't figure out if Teagan *knew* she had it in her (college, adulthood, all of it), even when we knew she did. About the stretch of evenings that suddenly felt both free and a little hollow.

There's this weird limbo between being co-parents and being a couple again. We still catch ourselves defaulting to kid talk: *Have you heard from her today? Did he send you that text, too?* Before remembering, oh right, this isn't a team huddle anymore. This is us.

Just us.

And that realization can feel disorienting. Even a little lonely. But also, and this is where our friends gave us some hope, it can be surprisingly tender. Like a second chance at something you forgot you used to be good at.

We're still figuring it out ourselves. Still stumbling over the new rhythm.

Some days we sync up easily. We finish each other's sentences, laugh at the same half-formed joke, and feel like a team.

Other days, well, other days we drift. We get quiet. Irritated. Disconnected in that vague, hard-to-name way. Like we forgot how to be a couple and started acting like co-managers of an overly quiet household.

But then there's a walk. Or a dance lesson. Or just two people on the couch, watching *Friends* reruns and remembering that kindness is brave, and belief is a muscle.

It's not always dramatic. Sometimes, rediscovery looks like a real conversation. Sometimes, it looks like folding laundry while your person talks about nothing in particular.

So, do we still like each other?

Most days, yes.

Some days, we feel it right away. Some days, we have to go looking for it. But so far, we're finding it.

And in this strange, tender season, that might not just be enough.

It might be the whole point.

5

We Thought We'd Be in Belize by Wednesday

We had this idea. Not a plan, definitely not a plan. But an idea. A fantasy that once the kids were out of the house, we'd just… go. Anywhere. Everywhere. That on any random Wednesday, one of us would say, "Belize?" and the other would already be halfway packed.

Turns out, that's not how this works.

We're still employed. Still paying tuition. Still needing PTO requests and Wi-Fi strong enough for Zoom. The Riverwalk in San Antonio? That's as spontaneous as it got this year. And even then, we had to wait for a weekend.

(Clancy will point out here, correctly, that empty nesting is not the same as retirement. But in Rick's head, the math somehow added up to permanent vacation.)

That's the thing about expectations; they sneak in like uninvited guests. You don't realize they're there until you're mildly annoyed that you're back at work on a Monday instead of sipping something with a tiny umbrella in it.

And expectation, it turns out, is a whole category of grief, joy, comedy, and awkward conversations. Like the one we had about how we thought we'd spend more time together. Real time. Candlelit dinners and deep talks and maybe some long, luxurious weekends of rediscovering each other.

What actually happened? We got home from our Riverwalk trip, Clancy went to the bedroom, Rick turned on football, and we didn't talk again until the Cowboys kicked off. And honestly, that was fine. More than fine. That was us doing us.

We both had to let go of the idea that "now that the kids are gone" meant instant reconnection. Like the parenting chapter would slam shut and we'd go skipping into Coupledom 2.0, holding hands and making out in grocery store aisles.

Spoiler: It doesn't work that way. (Also, the grocery store lighting is harsh. No one wants to make out near the freezer section.)

But the good stuff? It's there. It just looks different. It's a dumb inside joke from a road trip 27 years ago that still makes us laugh when we see an RV. It's learning to enjoy the quiet, like really enjoy it, even if one of us (Rick) takes a little longer to get comfortable in the silence. It's realizing we can cook whatever we want now because nobody's here to wrinkle their nose.

It's being together without having to be *on*.

That's maybe the biggest shift. You spend so long parenting, filling every silence with guidance or logistics or warnings about scams from the "Postal Service." And then one day, you're just sitting across from each other.

Just two people with a shared history, a shared couch, and the occasional tiff that dissolves after the first laugh.

So no, we haven't jetted off to Belize (yet). But we're learning to find the wonder in the unexpected shape of this season. The work it takes to reconnect. The freedom that's quieter and slower than we imagined. The joy of mismatched placemats and pizza nights and still quoting *Friends* like it's 1999.

And yes, we still talk about expectations. Mostly so we don't trip over them.

6

So... Who Am I Now?

Clancy

Okay, so here's the thing: I didn't expect to feel displaced. I don't even know if that's the right word. But after the kids left, there was this weird in-between space where I wasn't sure what role I was playing anymore.

I wasn't full-time "Mom" the way I used to be. I wasn't chauffeuring, checking grades, filling out camp forms, or curling anyone's hair before a game. (Teagan could totally do her own hair, but sometimes she just wanted me to do it. I loved that.)

Now, no one needs their hair curled. No one's asking what's for dinner before I even know what day it is. And suddenly, I'm not answering to anyone's schedule but my own.

Which should feel freeing, right?

And in a lot of ways, it does. There's joy in the small things, like cooking what *I* want. (Sloppy joes are back in the rotation. Sorry, Teagan.) But there's also this tug. Like I've lost one job, but I haven't figured out if, or how, I'm supposed to replace it.

I still teach fitness classes part-time, and I still care about it. But it doesn't sit on me the same way it used to. When the kids were home, the job felt heavier because it wasn't just about the people in my classes. It was about being home by a certain time, having enough energy left for dinner, for homework check-ins, for whatever crisis popped up at 9:00 p.m. It all overlapped.

Now, the work is still meaningful, but it takes up a different kind of space. I still want to do well, but I don't carry it around in the same way. There's less guilt, less scramble, fewer mental tabs open. My mind feels lighter, which is good, and weird.

And then there's this other thing. Little creative sparks that keep showing up, ideas I haven't had time or space for in years. I don't know where they're going yet (and no, I'm not ready to talk about them, even though Rick keeps trying to turn them into announcements). But something is shifting. Not a wholesale reinvention. Maybe just a resurfacing.

Because when you spend two decades answering to everyone else's needs, it's easy to forget what you even *like* doing. Who you are when no one's hungry. When no one needs reminding to send a thank-you note. When no one's coming through the door at four o'clock asking for a ride to Target.

So now I'm slowly figuring that out. Still taking care of us. Still holding the shape of a home. But also holding space for me, for the person I'm becoming.

Not the version of me from before the sign-ups and snack schedules and the endless hum of logistics.

Or maybe it is. But only in the sense that I've been shaped by all of that and now get to evolve in a new direction... not a returning to but a growing from.

And just when I start to worry that maybe the kids don't need me at all anymore, my phone rings. It's Teagan, walking home from the rec center. She doesn't *need* to call. She just *wants* to.

And yes, I'll always answer.

But then I hang up, and I write something down. I sit with a new idea. I cook something with zucchini because no one's here to pick it out. And I breathe into this strange, quiet, beautiful middle space between who I've been and who I might still become.

So, who am I now?

I don't fully know yet.

But I'm here for the unfolding.

7

We Haven't Touched a Thing

We always said we wouldn't be the kind of parents who turned their kid's bedroom into a home gym the second they left. And we haven't.

There was talk. A Pinterest board may have been created. (Clancy swears it was just to get ideas.) But the room is still exactly the same. Same bedding, same corkboard with old photos, same pile of "I might need this later" stuff that never made it to the dorm. It's all there, like a snapshot preserving a moment in time.

The truth is that it didn't feel right to change it. Not yet. Not while the leaving still feels temporary. Not while there are still Thanksgiving breaks and summer internships and weekends when she walks through the front door like she never left. We know she has one foot out the door, and that's exactly how it should be. But for now, we're choosing to let the room hold space for both things: the child who lived here and the adult who's figuring it out.

Still, something does shift. You walk past the door and think, *Is it still hers? Is it ours? Can it be neither?*

We laughed with friends recently about this: the way kids still expect to come home and have "their room," candles, trophies, jazz shoes, and all. And how we parents start eyeing the space differently, even if we never act on it. It's not about redecorating. It's about permission. Permission to admit we're entering a new chapter. Permission to wonder what might come next.

So no, we haven't changed anything. Not yet. But we might. Someday. Once it really feels like they're fully out and not just temporarily away.

And when that day comes, they'll still have a place to land.

Just maybe with new bedding.

8

Parenthood in Past Tense

Rick

Here's what no one tells you: Someday, the people who once needed you to cut their grapes into quarters will invite you to a bar you're too old to survive.

And not just any bar, a college bar. One with floors sticky enough to peel your shoes off and music loud enough to make you wonder if your hearing is finally going or if you're just not built for bass anymore.

We're heading to Arizona State for Parents' Weekend. Tanner's a senior now, which is a weird sentence to type. The kind of sentence that feels like it should come with a warning label: "Objects in mirror are closer to graduation than they appear." This is our fourth round of doing this: the tailgates, the off-campus sushi dinners, the halfhearted football games where we pretend to care about who ASU is playing. We don't. We're there for the nachos.

This year feels different. Not because he's changed (although he's twenty pounds heavier, ten of those in beard) but because we have. The ritual is now muscle memory. We land; we text him. He asks for a "cheeky grocery run," which I'm still not convinced is a real phrase, and then we head to Uncle Sal's for martinis. He meets us somewhere between dinner and midnight, and we get a few good hours of catch-up in before he disappears into the swarm of his life again.

We've become supporting characters in our son's story. Not the antagonists. Not the comic relief. Just the recurring guest stars. That's the role now. Show up. Smile. Pick up the tab.

It's not tragic. It's just weird. Like you're visiting the set of a show you used to star in.

And I say that with a strange mix of pride and longing. Watching Tanner do college life with ease (the confidence, the routine, the way he now orders dinner for the whole table like a middle-aged dad), it's like seeing the proof that all the effort worked. He's fine. He's more than fine. He's launched, which means, in a very real way, we've been laid off from the job of daily parenting.

But no one gives you a severance package for that. There's no ceremony where they hand you a plaque that says, "Thanks for the carpooling, the Band-Aids, and the algebra panic attacks."

You just stop being the center of their universe, and if you're lucky, you orbit close enough to catch a few texts, a cheeky grocery run, or a warm hug on the sidewalk before dinner.

9

We Said Yes...

We didn't plan to go full spring break. That's just what happened when we decided to say yes.

Yes to dinner at Houston's. Yes to Uncle Sal's. Yes to Casey Moore's Oyster House after Uncle Sal's. Yes to waiting in line for 45 minutes outside a place called Casa, where the drink of choice is served in literal plastic beach buckets.

(Yes, we had to clarify "buckets" did not mean a six-pack on ice. It meant something a toddler builds a sandcastle with, now filled with 32 ounces of college-kid margarita.)

But when your kid finally has the right ID to get into the places he used to walk past with a fake one and a backup story, you go.

You go, and you lean in.

It was senior year Parents' Weekend, and we knew this was the last one. The last time we'd fly in and try to keep up with kids who live on Red Bull and queso. The last round of meet-the-roommates, eat-all-the-things, try-not-to-be-too-obvious-as-you-tear-up-at-how-grown-they-are.

And somewhere between the bar line and the bottom of that oversized drink bucket, we just… let go.

We said yes to all of it.

So, yes to Casa, which felt like stepping into a music video for a song we didn't know. Yes to old tennis shoes (Clancy's suggestion), sticky floors, and shouting over blaring music while someone's vape cloud wafted our direction. Yes to walking back to the hotel like we were in our twenties—if our twenties had included ibuprofen and orthotics.

Yes, even to brunch the next morning. Yes to refilling the emotional tank just enough to do it all again that night.

It wasn't about the bars. Or the food. Or even the kids, really.

It was about us.

Saying yes, in that moment, was a kind of permission. Permission to be fully in it. Not sitting on the sidelines of their college life but sprinting toward the middle of it for one ridiculous, joyful weekend.

It was a celebration of who they're becoming and of who we're becoming now, too.

Because yes, this phase is different. Yes, there's grief tucked into the corners. But there's also joy. And laughter. And sometimes recovery mornings after sweaty, late-night, tequila-scented, slightly absurd benders with your adult adjacent kids.

And honestly?

We wouldn't trade it for anything.

10

The Art of Not Fixing It

We had plans for that Sunday. A recap breakfast. A little debrief in the car on the way to the airport. Maybe record something light for the podcast. We were riding that post-Parents' Weekend wave, still riding high from the tailgates, good meals, and watching Teagan shine in her new world.

Then she got in the car and started sobbing.

Like, *can't catch your breath, this is not about home-sickness* sobbing.

It hit us like a gut punch with a side of whiplash. One moment we're debating brunch orders, the next we're trying to figure out how to triage our daughter's emotional crisis from a parking lot.

We won't share the full details—it's her story, not ours—but let's just say: roommate conflict. The kind that crawls under your skin and sets up camp in your nervous system. And in that moment, every parenting reflex fired at once. We wanted to leap in. To solve it. To drive straight to the dorm and have a "mature conversation" with an 18-year-old we barely knew. To do something, anything, other than just sit there.

But she didn't need a rescue. She needed a release.

So we let her cry. We listened. We stayed quiet when it would've been easier to fill the space with mom fury or dad logic. (We considered both.) And when she finally exhaled, we hugged her goodbye and got on our flight home, feeling like we'd just left a part of ourselves behind in that car.

And then the texts started coming.

Clancy: I was already halfway through booking a flight before Rick gave me a look.

Rick: To be clear, it was a "how do we parent like adults now that our kid technically is one" look.

This was the moment. The one nobody really prepares you for when your child becomes an adult. The moment when she doesn't just need your protection or your presence. She needs your patience.

And wow, is that hard.

We've always thought we were pretty good at this. Giving them space. Letting them become who they are. But this was our first real test in the post-drop-off era. Not a packing-their-stuff or crying-in-the-Target-parking-lot kind of test.

This was emotional endurance. This was *don't fix it* parenting.

Which, for the record, is hard for any parent.

Rick: My instinct was to write a conflict-resolution checklist and email it to her.

Clancy: Mine was to call her RA. And her roommate's mom. And maybe an attorney for good measure.

We didn't do any of that. What we *did* do was listen. We asked if she wanted advice before giving any. We reminded her she was not alone. We prayed—hard. And we watched her handle it with more maturity and strength than we had any right to expect.

And this just might be the secret to parenting through this phase of life.

It's restraining the fixer, the fighter, the protector in you, and trusting the person you've raised.

It's remembering that you're not the captain of their ship anymore. You're more like a very committed lighthouse. Steady. Available. Pointing out the rocks but not steering the boat.

Rick: Also, occasionally screaming weather updates and offering snacks.

Clancy: Okay, *mostly* offering snacks.

In the end, they resolved it. Not perfectly. But peacefully. No one moved out in the middle of the night or set anything on fire, which, in college roommate terms, is a major win. They talked. They compromised on a short-term solution and agreed to different long-term living arrangements.

But more importantly, Teagan did it. On her terms. With her voice. And in her time.

We're still learning how to parent adult children. It's trial and error. Some days, it's holding your breath. Some days, it's holding your tongue. And some days, if you're lucky, it's holding back just enough to watch them rise.

11

Of Course It Happened on a Trip

We didn't stumble into being travel people; we designed it that way. From the very beginning, we've been dreaming, planning, and packing for the next trip. Travel has always been part of our individual DNA, but together, it became one of the foundational pieces of "us." We weren't just falling in love; we were booking flights, mapping routes, and building a relationship around the joy (and occasional chaos) of being somewhere new.

It all started with a "just friends" weekend in New Hampshire.

Clancy: I was still in college, Rick was already in the work world, and we genuinely thought we were just friends. Or at least that's what we told everyone, including ourselves. He invited me to New Hampshire to hike, hang out, and breathe fresh air. I told my parents, "Hey, I'm flying to New Hampshire to meet this guy you haven't met yet!" They were skeptical.

Rick: I want it on the record that I had *zero* ulterior motives. There just weren't many hotels where I was working, and a bed and breakfast seemed practical. Breakfast included. I'd planned for efficiency, not seduction.

Clancy: Sure. Except then we had this very unintentionally romantic, candlelit dinner at that cute place in the woods. Then it started to rain, and the innkeeper drove us home through the dark, wet forest after it poured. I remember calling our friend Jennifer that night and saying, "So, I think we're a couple now."

That trip was the launchpad. And from then on, our relationship unfolded across airports and off-ramps.

Rick: If there's a unifying theme in our early years, it was travel-induced problem solving. Like Clancy arriving in New York with no toiletries because her friend Jennifer sped off in her purple Geo loaner before she realized the bag was still in the backseat. Or the camping trip where raccoons stole our s'mores before we even roasted them. Or the time we almost capsized a canoe in Caddo Lake because I spotted a very healthy-sized snake.

Clancy: There are rules now, like we don't camp unless there's a real bathroom. And "rustic" means a boutique hotel with sub-200 thread count sheets.

Rick: But in between the mishaps, we built something. Our honeymoon in Antigua was pure magic. The kind of magic that includes European beach-goers who maybe should've packed more fabric. But also the kind where the bed was lofted to catch the ocean view, and every dinner felt like a date we'd waited years to have.

Clancy: And Hawaii, for our first anniversary, we said we weren't in a rush to have kids. And then, under the stars, with ocean air and a very nice bottle of wine, I told Rick I was ready to try. Three months later, Tanner was on the way.

Rick: Of course, we would decide to start a family on a trip. It's just what we do.

But not every trip was dreamy. Years later, we took a very different kind of trip to Arizona. Not to celebrate but to salvage. We were in a hard place. The kind where you're not quite saying the word "divorce," but you're wondering if you're drifting too far apart to find each other again.

Clancy: That trip was a lifeline. We had miles, points, and willing grandparents to watch the kids. We needed space to talk without dishes in the sink, carpools, or conference calls.

Rick: We went back recently to the same restaurant where we had some of those big, hard conversations. It's become a sacred space for us now. Proof that you can repair something if you both still care enough to try.

Travel didn't save our marriage. But it did give us a place to see each other more clearly. To zoom out from the mess and remember the magic.

Clancy: It's funny now, looking back. All those trips we took before the kids. Then with the kids. And now, after the kids.

Rick: We still build memories. Still chase a view, a meal, a moment.

Clancy: And we still have rules. No camping. Plenty of snacks. And if there's a snake, I'm out.

12

Hi, My Name Is Clancy, and I Love TV

Clancy

I've loved TV since I was a little girl. That probably sounds like a confession, but I don't actually feel bad about it. Not really. I mean, I'm also a reader. I'll prop myself up in bed and dig into a book like it's my job, which, to be clear, it's not. Mostly novels, mostly for escape, and sometimes, I stay up way too late because I *have* to know what happens next. But when it comes down to it, TV has always been one of my love languages.

I watched soaps with my mom. *The Young and the Restless,* if we're naming names. And yes, I still keep up with it. My friend's Aunt Sherry and I send Facebook messages back and forth like it's breaking news. And every time the kids come home, they walk in, see Victor on screen, and ask the same question, "Is he dead yet?" He's not. He never is.

TV is comfort food for me. Familiar. Predictable in the best way. It's what I turn to when I want to unwind, when I want to laugh, when I just want something to anchor the room. Rick wasn't a big TV person early in our marriage. He'd watch a few things, but he didn't love it the way I did. Not until the pandemic, anyway. That's when the rest of the world caught up with binge-watching, and I finally brought Rick over to the dark side. Not just "sit in the same room and scroll your phone" watching. Actual together-together watching.

And let me tell you, there's something weirdly intimate about sitting next to someone in silence while you both fall in love with the same fictional people. Or hate-watch the same terrible show. (Looking at you, *Manifest.*)

We've had whole seasons of our marriage marked by what we were watching. Thursday nights used to be *Friends* and *Seinfeld* and a frozen pizza after Tanner's bath. We'd tape it on the VCR and press play like it was our own tiny ritual. Those nights were our date nights.

Now we have streaming apps and skip-intro buttons, and neither of us would dare watch ahead. But it still feels like us. Like a continuation of something sweet we started when we were young, tired, and covered in bath toys.

Some nights, we quote *Seinfeld* like it's Shakespeare. Some nights, we try something new and end up watching with one eye while folding laundry. Sometimes, we commit to finishing a show we no longer enjoy just because we started it.

I think that's part of the beauty of this phase. The kids are out of the house. The rooms are quiet. But the TV is on. And not just as background noise but as something that holds a little piece of our history, our humor, our connection.

So yeah. Hi, my name is Clancy, and I love TV. And I love what it's given us, too.

13

The Cure for Happiness

We should've known it was going to be one of those weeks when the TV blew up. Not metaphorically. Not "it went out" or "stopped working." No, we're talking full-blown, cat-leaps-off-your-lap, dramatic *Pop!* followed by sudden screen death.

Now, we have other TVs. We're not exactly off the grid. But that was our couch-TV. Our "this is where we decompress together" screen. And that night, with the house too quiet and the weather too chilly and the energy just off, it hit harder than it should have.

Rick had just gotten back from his haircut place (the one that gives you a bourbon when you walk in, which is either genius marketing or a trap). Clancy met him at the door with, "Go pour another. You're gonna need it."

That should've been our clue: The vibes were shifting.

Then the call came.

Rick: I don't usually get the first call. That's Clancy's domain. She's the emotional triage nurse; I'm more the post-op guy with the clipboard. But this time, it was me. Tanner called just after I'd finished a meeting.

It was one of those conversations where the parent in you wants to fix it, but you realize you can't.

He'd just hit a big disappointment. One of those milestone rejections that punctuate early adulthood. It wasn't a catastrophe. Just a door that didn't open the way he'd hoped. The kind that stings more because he actually *tried*. He put in the work. He aimed high. And then, *thud*.

Tanner's one of those kids who has always seemed to land on his feet. It's not that he hasn't worked hard—he has—but for most of his life, the sun just seemed to shine where he stood. This time, the clouds rolled in. And he felt it.

Clancy: By the time he called me, he'd already spiraled a bit. Which, honestly, fair. He's a senior, trying to line up what comes next, and suddenly, everyone else's plans look shinier and simpler. His friends are getting job offers and signing leases. He's staring down three more years of school and doesn't even know what zip code that school will be in.

He started piling on about the rejection, about Japanese class being too hard, about everything. And I listened. And then I did that mom thing where you accidentally turn into a mirror. I said, "Well, yeah. You've been enjoying your life. You're not locking yourself in the library on Friday nights like your sister. You're out. You're living. That's not bad. But let's not pretend you've been grinding nonstop."

That probably wasn't what he wanted to hear, but he took it. And I hope, eventually, it helped.

Rick: It's weird doing this from a distance. When he was younger and the world went sideways, we could hug it out. Take him for ice cream. Distract, comfort, do. Now we're parenting via phone lines, text threads, and care packages from Insomnia Cookies or fried pickle money.

(Yes, fried pickles. Apparently, they are, according to Tanner, "the cure to happiness." We think he means *the secret to happiness,* so we Venmoed him enough for a round or two at his favorite pub. It's not a hug. But it's something.)

Clancy: That's the hard part about this stage. You're still their safety net, but it's a *relational* one, not a physical one. You don't get to swoop in with cookies and a blanket. You just hope your words land. And maybe a little Rangers win helps, too.

Rick: Tanner's a "next play" kid. I love that about him. When I was in consulting, everyone talked about making partner like it was the holy grail. But I looked around and saw a lot of tan lines where wedding rings used to be. That grind isn't always worth it. So maybe this setback trims the options that don't really serve him anyway. Maybe this is one of those weird gifts that shows up dressed like failure.

Clancy: I told him that, too. Well, not the tan lines. But that you usually end up where you're meant to be. Even if you don't recognize it at first. His college wasn't even on our radar. Now he loves it. Sometimes, the closed door reroutes you toward something better. And sometimes, it just sucks for a bit before it makes sense.

Rick: And we keep learning that as parents, too. That being a support system now means biting your tongue, asking instead of advising, and knowing when all they really need is a listening ear. (Even if we're secretly making a list of solutions they didn't ask for.)

Clancy: That list is real. And it takes all my energy not to send it.

We're figuring it out as we go: how to parent from the bleachers instead of the field. How to show up without showing up uninvited. How to send a long-distance hug and trust it reaches them.

Some days, it's a text. Some days, it's a bar tab and a fried appetizer. And some days, it's just picking up the phone when they call.

14

Table for Eight, Please

We didn't expect Halloween to become our favorite adult holiday, but there we were. No costumes, no candy bowl, no kids. Just eight adults, a round of margaritas, and the strange pleasure of being seated immediately at Salsa, our go-to Tex-Mex spot that normally requires a blood sacrifice to get a table on a Tuesday.

Halloween had always been chaos in the best way. Candy buckets, neighborhood meetups, the wagon parade down the street. For 21 years, we were all-in. And now, nothing. For the first time in over two decades, we didn't buy a single fun-size anything.

Clancy: "I did cave and grab a clearance bag afterward."

Rick: "Because it felt weird not to. And also, KitKat bars."

So, instead of sitting on our porch waiting for the doorbell to ring, we went to dinner with our old trick-or-treat crew. And not a single sticky-fingered toddler in sight.

There's this weird perk of empty nesting you don't realize until you get here: You get to do things when everyone else is busy parenting, like traveling in September. Or, apparently, going out to dinner on Halloween and feeling like you have the whole town to yourself.

We sat there for hours, ordering a second round of margaritas, laughing with the same friends who used to huddle with us under fleece blankets on the driveway. But this time, no one was rushing home for bedtime. No one was monitoring candy trades or counting how many peanut butter cups made it into the bag.

And it was wonderful.

We didn't realize until that night how much we'd been bracing ourselves for this first empty nest holiday. It felt like another small loss, another reminder that the house was changing. But instead, it turned into something sweet (and not the fun-size kind).

We'll probably buy candy next year. Maybe leave the porch light on, just in case. But now we know Halloween doesn't have to be a grief trigger. It can be what we make it. It can be tacos instead of candy bowls. A table for eight instead of a driveway full of wagons.

And that feels like the start of a new tradition.

PART II

Winter

15

Turkey in Tucson

This year, we took Thanksgiving to Arizona, Tempe and Tucson, to be exact. Two cities, two kids, one shared rental car, and approximately one million pies. (Okay, maybe four, but still.)

We'd planned the whole thing like it was a heist. Flights, rental cars, catering orders, and game tickets. There were spreadsheets. Backup plans. A grocery store run that nearly ended our marriage. (Clancy: "You want to go to Costco on *Tuesday* before Thanksgiving?" Rick: "Liquor. And pie.")

Spoiler: We did go to Costco. And Trader Joe's. And Albertsons. And somehow, it was kind of lovely? Not the chaos we'd braced for. Just regular folks being quietly competent in a parking lot that threatened to eat our rental car whole.

On Wednesday, we hiked Saguaro National Park. The east side, this time. The one with the flatter trails and that bone-deep silence. At one point, we saw horseback riders in the distance, but other than that, not another human in sight. There was something holy about that kind of silence. The kind that doesn't ask anything of you.

It was probably our last moment of tranquility before the tidal wave of turkey logistics.

The catered meal turned out to be fully refrigerated. Every dish needed cooking. Surprise! But the Airbnb had two ovens, and Clancy channeled her inner NASA engineer to coordinate reheat timing like a moon landing.

The turkey was a disaster. Four pounds of sadness. But the biscuits were amazing. And the mac and cheese was perfect. And honestly, no one cried over the bird. Except maybe Clancy, silently, while smiling through a mouthful of mashed potatoes.

After dinner, Teagan offered her review of the Costco pecan pie: "It's fine. But it's not angry." Apparently, her best pies are made when she's mad. Rage-baked crusts and cathartic cinnamon. We missed the fury this year but gained the sweet, strange comfort of store-bought ease.

We played Phase 10. We suspected Tanner and Teagan's BiBi (Clancy's mom) was cheating. Got called out in Round Two. We laughed until our faces hurt.

Later that night, Tanner's friends came over, one of them a self-declared Phase 10 purist, and suddenly, we were deep in a multi-generational debate over house rules, wild cards, and whether you *really* have to discard to go out.

By the time the rivalry game hit on Saturday, Arizona vs. Arizona State, we were ready. Sunscreen in our pockets, tickets in hand, house-divided shirts on our backs. Tanner left before halftime. His team was losing. Teagan beamed. Life moved.

And then, on Sunday, it got quiet again.

A Target run. Airport drop-offs. A long walk around a nearly empty campus, the kind of walk you take not to get somewhere but just to feel a place one more time.

We sat at the Tucson airport bar in near silence. Not in a sad way. Just used up. The way you feel when you've done the thing you set out to do. When the words run out, but your heart is full.

16

We Tried 30 Empty Nester Dates So You Don't Have To

We didn't set out to test 30 empty-nester date ideas in one sitting. It started, as many things do these days, with a Google search and a bit of desperation.

We needed content for the podcast. (That's Clancy's line. Rick would call it "structure.") Either way, it was one of those "what are we even doing this weekend?" moments. So Clancy stumbled across a blog post: "30 Fun and Flirty Date Ideas for Empty Nesters."

Which, okay, "fun and flirty" is doing a lot of heavy lifting there.

But we were curious. How many had we done? How many would we actually want to do? And what does it say about us that we have strong opinions about museum lighting, grocery store lists, and whether biking counts as a good time?

Turns out, quite a bit.

Hiking

We've done this one. Multiple times. Sometimes with just the two of us, sometimes with a kid in tow, which breaks the empty nest vibe but fills a different kind of cup. One of our favorite memories now comes from a hike where Rick, convinced he'd found a shortcut, led us on a route that was neither short nor remotely a cut. After that, Clancy started saying, "Let's not get Utah-ed," and the phrase stuck. It means, "Don't let him make it harder than it needs to be."

And that might be our new motto for this phase of life.

Dancing

The idea of two-stepping under string lights? Yes, please. But it can't be the glitzy kind of country dancing. We're talking sawdust on the floor, country music hall vibes, maybe a little George Strait in the background. Rick even Googled where to find that kind of place. (If you know, help us out. North Texas recommendations welcome.)

Clancy prefers a group class to private lessons. Rick prefers not feeling like a neon sign in a room full of 22-year-olds. So we'll keep looking for our kind of scene. Something with rhythm and reasonable lighting.

Picnics, Museums, and Grocery Store Dates

We have feelings. Lots of them.

Picnics? Lovely in theory. In practice, we don't want to pack that much stuff. We'd rather pick up sandwiches and call it a win.

Museums? Yes, but only with limited square footage and decent benches. We have an art threshold.

Grocery store as a date? That's a hard no. It's not cute. It's not romantic. It's Clancy with a list and Rick tossing in Cheez-Its and pleading for two-bite brownies. We've tried it. The marriage survived. Barely.

Pottery Classes and Painting Nights

You could not pay Clancy to do this again. Somewhere under our bed is a canvas with a pine tree that looks like it was painted mid-earthquake. She still has flashbacks to the Painting With a Twist era.

Rick, ever the optimist, brought up the movie *Ghost*. He was shut down immediately.

Live Theater and Cooking Classes

These are yeses. Especially when they involve friends. Cooking with Poo in Thailand (yes, that was the actual name) remains one of our all-time favorite travel memories. Not because we became culinary geniuses but because we laughed the entire time and still talk about it.

Theater is trickier. We like it. We don't like committing to a whole Broadway series just to get the one show we actually want to see. But small, local productions? That might be our sweet spot.

Bowling, Games, and Impulsive Gatherings

Here's where we shine.

We're not trying to join a league, but bowling with friends? Absolutely. (The article mentioned something about a "sexy twist" on bowling, called *bedroom bowling*, which... no thank you. We're fun, but we're not *that* fun.)

Game night with just the two of us? We're working on it. (TV is Clancy's first love, but Rick's trying to make room for a little friendly competition.)

And unplanned, impulsive gatherings? That's our love language. Text friends two hours before, tell them to bring something, and end up making break-fast tacos at midnight. That's our version of hosting.

So what did we learn?

We're not reinventing our marriage in the empty nest. We're remembering it. Rediscovering what made us laugh, what still makes us curious, and what we forgot we used to love doing together.

Some of these ideas were ridiculous. Some were surprisingly sweet. A few were already part of our lives. But the best part was sitting together, laughing about it all, and realizing we still want to try things. Still want to play.

Even if we skip the bedroom bowling, whatever that means. (Seriously, we're still confused.)

17

"Bye, Buddy. Hope You Find Your Dad."

We spotted it in Forever 21. A bright blue sweatshirt with a narwhal and the words: "Bye, Buddy. Hope you find your dad." Clancy gasped and pointed like she'd seen a celebrity. The sweater was already sold out in her size. Of course it was. But still, she stood there in the middle of the store whispering, "Hope you find your dad," like a prayer to the Elf gods.

This is the first holiday season without either kid home yet. The house is decorated, the lights are up, the cat is traumatized, and we're bingeing our favorite Christmas movies like the kids *are* home. It feels different.

We used to squeeze movie nights in between football games, school projects, and end-of-semester chaos. Now, it's Tuesday night, and we're watching *Four Christmases* for the second time this week, quoting Vince Vaughn like it's totally normal.

Clancy: "You just gonna stare at me while you eat those wings?"

Rick: "I can't look at it. I can't."

We say it every single time our daughter has to clean up after her cat barfs. Every. Time. She rolls her eyes so hard they might get stuck, but underneath the exasperation, there's this tiny flicker of amusement, which just means we nailed it.

And yes, we've quoted *Four Christmases* walking into church. Not on purpose. But it slips out. (We're not saying which scene. It involves Dwight Yoakam, clapping, and Vince Vaughn. That's all you need to know.)

The point is, these movies live with us. They've taken root. They show up like second nature, quotes, callbacks, and eyerolls included.

We have shirts from *Christmas Vacation*. We wore them to a private theater we rented during COVID so everyone could safely spread out and quote Cousin Eddie in surround sound. Clancy's shirt: "Why is the carpet all wet, Todd?" Rick's: "I don't know, Margo." Tanner's? Let's just say it featured Cousin Eddie's most iconic line and the reason we kept him seated in the back row.

There was the year we found the *Elf* snowball fight bridge in Central Park. The kids recreated the scene, even without snow. Another year, we watched *Prep & Landing* (a cute little cartoon about elves prepping houses for Santa) and somehow ended up in a full-blown debate about logistical elf operations. Rooftop access, global time zones, chain of command. You know, normal stuff.

Even the classics evolve. Rick, who once shrugged off *It's a Wonderful Life* as a black-and-white nap opportunity, now, as an adult, has a better understanding of George Bailey. The weight he carries. The ache of trying to do right and wondering if it matters. The slow doubt that creeps in when no one's looking. "Strange, isn't it? Each man's life touches so many other lives."

And then there's *Frosty*. Our version is a six-minute short film. We play it until the audio glitch in the scene when the kids are naming Frosty. It cracks our family up every time; other families might not even notice it. We don't even finish the movie anymore. Why would we? The joke *is* the tradition.

Which brings us to the great cultural divide: *Is Die Hard a Christmas movie?*

Around here, that question isn't up for discussion. Teagan has settled it.

One year, seemingly out of nowhere, she announced *Die Hard* was her favorite Christmas movie. We didn't see that coming. But suddenly, it was her thing. Now she insists it's playing while we bake pies, and our Christmas isn't complete until Bruce Willis says a thing we're not allowed to print here.

What we're learning is that traditions don't have to be performed perfectly to matter. You don't need everyone physically present to feel connected. Memory, repetition, and a shared laugh across states or screens? That counts.

Next week, they'll be home. We'll rewatch everything with them, even if we just watched it two days ago. The movies aren't the point. They never were. It's the rhythm. The quoting. The way we all know when to laugh before the line is even delivered.

So yes, the house is quieter this year. But the traditions? Loud as ever.

18

Friday Night Mixtape

Remember mixtapes?

Not playlists, actual mixtapes.

You had to earn those. Sitting by the stereo with a finger on the record button, hoping no one talked over the intro. And when you listened, you couldn't skip around. You just let it play in order. You lived with it.

There's something about that: how the meaning wasn't just in the songs but in the way they were stitched together. The mood they made. The chapter they held. The moment they captured.

Somewhere along the way, our Friday nights started to feel like that.

Track 1: Slumber Parties and Pizza Slices

Clancy: Every Friday in elementary school, someone was sleeping over. It wasn't a big deal. You just asked in the hallway, and someone ended up at your house with a Little Caesars pizza in that giant paper sleeve. We'd rip it open like it was a scroll of joy.

Rick: Or we'd be camped out with an Atari at a friend's house. I remember being so excited to play on a 5200 one weekend that it was basically a religious experience. Add Blockbuster into the mix, sometimes waiting for someone to return the movie you *really* wanted, and Fridays felt infinite.

Clancy: And unparented. We'd toilet paper houses and think we were *criminal masterminds*. My dad's only system of surveillance was a light over the sink. If it was still on when he woke up, someone was getting a lecture.

Rick: My dad tried something similar, which I interpreted, at the time, as a massive vote of no confidence. Now, I totally get it. He just wanted to know I hadn't been kidnapped from a keg party out on 2222.

Track 2: Live Music and Per Diems

Rick: When we were dating, Fridays felt like jailbreak. I was consulting, flying back and forth every week, and Clancy was finishing school and working hospital shifts.

Clancy: I'd come straight from the hospital in my scrubs, hair in a clip, still half in nurse mode. Sometimes, I'd already be at your apartment before you got back. Other times, we'd meet up in Deep Ellum. We basically lived there on weekends.

Rick: We had no money, but we somehow ate like we did, thanks to my per diem. I'd live off sad airport food during the week so we could go to actual restaurants when I got home.

Clancy: It was a weird combo of grown-up and completely broke. Like, fancy dinner, but we split everything and parked five blocks away to save $10.

Rick: And then we'd go back to the apartment, sit on the couch, put on music, and just *be*. No TV.

Clancy: Well, except sports.

Rick: Right. Sports don't count. That's *cultural enrichment*.

Clancy: Later, when I started flying as a flight attendant, the travel part of Fridays got even wilder. Remember the last-minute trip to Kansas City? And that one time you came with me on a flight when I got called out during Christmas Eve service?

Rick: Oh, yeah. That Southwest standby life.

Clancy: I think that phase taught us how to *move* together, like, literally and metaphorically. We were figuring it out: how to be a team, how to find each other in the middle of busy lives. Fridays were kind of our reset button.

Track 3: The Chili's Years

Rick: Fridays with little kids were an adventure. We'd go out to eat just to feel human again, and inevitably, one of them would blow chunks mid-meal.

Clancy: For some reason, always at Chili's. I have been barfed on in almost every Chili's in the state of Texas. That's not an exaggeration.

Rick: And always on you.

Clancy: Yep. That's the kind of thing you remember when your "Friday night out" involves diaper bags and kids in car seats.

Rick: We still tried, though. We swapped baby-sitting with friends, joined a supper club, and called in Clancy's parents for backup. We fought for date nights because we needed them.

Clancy: And then came sports.

Rick: Oh yeah, phase two of the parenting mixtape. Competitive soccer, competitive cheer, competitive *everything*.

Clancy: Suddenly, Fridays weren't about date nights; they were about getting uniforms clean and making sure we had enough snacks to survive a weekend tournament.

Rick: We'd be up at 6:00 a.m. doing cheer hair or packing coolers for soccer fields. And forget eating out. You couldn't even *think* about dinner plans when you knew you had to be an hour and a half away at sunrise.

Clancy: I remember looking at families at restaurants at 5:00 p.m. and thinking, *Why are they eating so early?* And now I know, because they're us.

Rick: We became those people. Dinner at 5:00. Home by 8:00.

Clancy: And cocktails at home because, hey, at least we could make those strong.

Rick: That's the thing, our Friday nights weren't really ours anymore. They belonged to the kids, their schedules, their activities. We just found little ways to hold onto each other in the middle of it all.

Track 4: Reclaiming the Playlist

Rick: Now? Now, our Fridays start at 3:30, and we are not sorry.

Clancy: We have a place called The Owl. It's our spot. We sit, we sip, we exhale. And by the time we're home, we have time to digest *and* stream a show before 9:00 p.m. Empty nest, baby.

Rick: We could've defaulted to doing nothing, to saying, "Oh well, we're tired." But we didn't. We decided to *choose* our Fridays again.

Clancy: And now that the kids are in college, the calendar has room again. Sure, it fills up fast when they're home, but when it's just us, we're finding rhythm. Routine. Romance, even.

Rick: That's the thing about midlife. You've heard every track. You've lived through the noise. Now, you get to *curate* what plays. But if you'd told me 20 years ago that our "wild" Friday nights would someday involve early dinners and leftovers for Sunday lunch, I probably would've panicked.

Clancy: And now, it feels like freedom. Like, we finally get to choose.

We used to just take what Fridays gave us.

Whatever came on the "radio" of life—late nights, early mornings, chaos, curfews—we let it roll. Some songs we loved, some we tolerated, and a few we'd fast-forward if we could.

Now, we get to be deliberate. We know what we want to play. We leave room for surprises, but we're not afraid to skip what doesn't fit anymore.

19

Fa La La Full Nest

We'd been empty nesters for months, and then suddenly, overnight, the house was full again. Suitcases dumped in the entryway, shoes in every corner, music (and arguments about music) bleeding through the walls. There was a moment, somewhere between the airport pickup and the first load of laundry, when we looked at each other and thought, *Oh, right, this is what a full house feels like.*

It was the first time both kids had been home together since August. They'd finished finals. Teagan had zero commitments looming. Tanner didn't have to check in with professors. It was like the universe gave us the rarest of gifts: time without a to-do list.

And we tried to savor it.

Rick even said, out loud, that he *sat still and appreciated.* For him, that's basically a TED Talk. Normally, he's the one glancing at his watch, making a mental list of the next thing to tackle, already moving three steps ahead. But this time, he just stopped. No rush, no "I should be doing something productive." He sat, looked around at the kids sprawled on the couch, the Christmas lights still twinkling in the background, and actually let himself take it in.

There were nights we all went out and nights we just hung in the same room together, everyone doing their own thing: one kid on a laptop, another scrolling, us half-watching a movie. Nothing particularly special was happening. But somehow, that "nothing special" felt exactly right, like the point wasn't to create a perfect moment. The point was to be in the moment we already had.

We cooked. (Okay, *Clancy* cooked. Rick mostly "supervised" from a safe distance.) We hit the kids' favorite restaurants. We finally took the pictures we never seem to have time for when everyone's racing in different directions. And yes, there was the inevitable holiday chaos: schedules to coordinate, dishes piled high, someone yelling about who left the kitchen a disaster (also Clancy, but with good reason). But even in the mess, we knew we were lucky.

Maybe it was because we'd been living in a quiet house for so long, but the full nest felt lighter this time. We weren't reverting to old "mom and dad" roles. The kids had their lives; we had ours. We even snuck out a few nights for dinners and parties of our own. Clancy still caught herself double-checking what the kids were doing before we left, while Rick had apparently "moved on." (Clancy's version: *I just care about our children.* Rick's version: *I'm fine letting them be actual adults.* Both true. Both slightly annoying to the other.)

One night, Teagan asked Clancy to make her broccoli cheese soup, the one she swears "just tastes like home," and Tanner requested Tuscan chicken, one of those "real meals" that apparently don't happen in his apartment. There's something about a kid asking for *your* recipes that makes you feel ten feet tall. Even if those recipes involve a crockpot and take ten minutes, it's still love served on a plate.

Not that it all turned out picture-perfect. There was the pie incident when Clancy, without realizing it, used self-rising flour and ended up with crusts that floated to the top like upside-down cake. Years ago, that would've been a meltdown. This year, we laughed and ate it anyway. (Pro tip: Pecan pie tastes the same even when it's structurally unsound.)

And yes, there were heavier parts, too. We made our annual trip to Austin after Christmas, and the visit to Rick's mom's memory care was its usual cocktail of grief and grace. She's in the deepest stages of Alzheimer's now. We don't know how much she knows or if she recognizes us at all. It's horrible. It's sad. But we've learned to make it light where we can, telling stories, cracking jokes, laughing when she yawns every time Rick starts talking.

Rick: "I like to think it's a coincidence."
Clancy: "It's not."

We've learned to laugh where we can because the alternative is to let the grief swallow you whole.

We also visited Rick's 99-year-old Nana, who still lives independently and can text better than most 20-year-olds. Standing in her kitchen, where she's ordered groceries online since before it was cool, was a reminder of the full arc of family. Kids home from college. Parents growing older. Grandparents holding on to independence with both hands. It's a lot to hold, all at once.

By New Year's Eve, the full house had emptied again. Tanner was in Phoenix at an EDM festival (think rave at a NASCAR track). Teagan had friends over upstairs. We, meanwhile, were at home in our pajamas, bourbons in hand, watching Anderson Cooper on CNN and a segment about a cat café in Tokyo. Miso perked up at the TV and tried to paw the screen, convinced he'd discovered new friends.

There was a time when we felt obligated to be out late on nights like that, but these days, we're happy to be in. Pizza on the coffee table. Ringing in the new year our way.

The next morning, the house felt quiet. We made black-eyed peas, a nod to tradition, and texted Tanner to confirm he'd survived the rave. Teagan drifted in and out with her friends. We let the day be slow.

That's the thing we're learning about this phase of life: the loud doesn't cancel the quiet, and the quiet doesn't cancel the loud. They can sit side by side, just like grief and joy, just like chaos and contentment.

Postscript

Both my mom and Nana have passed since the time of this story. There's a tenderness in looking back now at the chaos, the laughter, the small moments that felt ordinary then but feel sacred now. We're grateful for all of it, and for them.

20

Micro-Enhancements and Other Middle-Life Myths

We've never been big "New Year's resolution" people. Something about announcing a dramatic personal reinvention over a bowl of queso on December 31 just feels doomsday adjacent. But still, there's something about a clean calendar with those blank little boxes that whispers, *You could be someone new this year.* Or at least someone who drinks more water and less wine.

(Rick would like to point out that we *did* try dry January once. It lasted until about January 12, possibly 8.)

But this year, Teagan gave us a better phrase. She said she doesn't do resolutions; she makes goals. And then *The New York Times* chimed in with an even better term: micro-enhancements. Not a total overhaul. Just a little fine-tuning. A nudge toward who you already are, but slightly more hydrated.

We like that. It feels right for where we are: second-semester empty nesters. Not newbies anymore, but definitely not seniors in this stage either. Maybe we have a decent GPA, but we still sometimes forget our lunch.

So, here are a few of our micro-enhancements for the year:

Clancy:

1. **Say yes more often.** No more hiding behind the "well, we've got a kid thing that night" excuse.

2. **Get creative.** Less screen time. More brain time. (This one will be hard. She loves her shows.)

3. **Clear the closets.** Literally, it's starting to look like a time capsule in there. Poor Teagan tried to find a childhood book and opened a door to Narnia.

Rick:

1. **Reshape the business.** Optimizing for flexibility over hustle. And hopefully, a little more purpose baked in. It's not just about making money; it's about serving well.

2. **Finally take that camping trip.** The Guadalupe Mountains aren't going to hike themselves.

3. **Eat more cheese.** (Micro, but important.)

We're not calling these resolutions because we want them to last past Super Bowl weekend. We're not expecting enlightenment. Just small shifts. Course corrections. Acts of gentle reinvention.

We're realizing that midlife isn't a mountain to summit. It's a series of weird little hills. Some you climb. Some you coast. Some you sit on with a glass of wine and say, "Huh. I didn't expect to like this view."

Maybe that's the real myth of middle life: that it's supposed to be a straight path. That after the kids leave, you either grieve dramatically or reinvent yourself in a blaze of yoga and vision boards. But the truth, at least for us, has been quieter. Gentler. Sometimes funny. Sometimes hard. Often both at once.

21

Empty Nester Questions

It started with one of those evenings where nothing was technically wrong, but something felt off. Dinner was fine (leftovers, eaten on the couch). The house was quiet, not in a peaceful way, but in a "did we forget something?" way. We hadn't. The kids were gone. The calendar was empty. And we were staring at each other like, *Okay, now what?*

So Clancy did what any modern woman with a Wi-Fi signal and a slightly restless heart would do: She Googled.

"Questions empty nesters should ask each other."
Not exactly poetry, but it got us somewhere.

We found a list. Ten prompts for couples entering this weird, wonderful, occasionally wobbly next chapter. We picked five.

What's One Country You'd Like to Visit Together?

This one felt easy. A softball. We'd talked about travel a lot before kids, during kids, in those five-minute windows when no one needed us and we remembered we were married.

Rick went big, Maldives big. Overwater bungalows, impossible blue water, and a "let's do this before the ocean swallows it" urgency.

Clancy picked Greece. Beauty, history, food, a little walking, a little lounging. A trip with both sun and substance.

We weren't surprised by each other's answers. But we did both pause at the realization that we were still picturing a future *together*. And the idea that there are still firsts ahead: new places, new stories, new versions of "us" we haven't met yet.

What Do You Need From Me Now?

Clancy said accountability. Rick's eyebrows did a thing. Clancy clarified: not drill sergeant-level, just a little gentle prodding. There are things she wants to start, and motivation in winter is not exactly her spiritual gift.

Rick said encouragement and involvement, especially in some of the creative ideas this next season might hold. Not the spreadsheets-and-consulting kind of work. The what-if-we-actually-built-something-together kind.

We realized, halfway through talking, that we'd said the same thing in different dialects. Clancy used "accountability." Rick said "affirmation." Both were just another way of saying: *Be in this with me. Nudge me. See me. Believe in the thing I want to do, even if I haven't done it yet.*

How Would You Like Our Sex Life to Change?

We didn't flinch. (You can't really podcast with someone after 24 years of marriage without a little TMI immunity.)

Rick leaned toward flirtatiousness. Spontaneity. More of the *before-kids* vibe when connection wasn't sandwiched between laundry cycles and ACT prep.

Clancy leaned toward intimacy. Not just *the thing*, but *the leading up to the thing*. Touches that aren't task-oriented. The kind of closeness that's less about green lights and more about being known.

Again, we found the overlap. Different angles. Same desire: *Let's make room for connection, not just logistics.*

Any New Hobbies You Want to Try?

Let's just say our answers were not entirely aligned.

Clancy: Pickleball (when it's not freezing) and, weirdly, closet organization (which apparently counts if you treat it like a hobby and not a cry for help.)

Rick: Golf. (Clancy made a face.) And two-stepping. (Clancy made a different face.)

Turns out we're still learning what makes the other person light up. And just like in year one of marriage, some of those things may require negotiation, and good footwear.

Describe a Perfect Retired Day

The funny part? We couldn't even picture one fully. But we could feel it.

It's the absence of alarms. It's a slow morning. Tea that isn't rushed. Maybe a workout. Maybe a walk. Maybe a late breakfast at a place we've passed a hundred times but never had time to try.

It's not doing *everything* together, but still having the time and energy to *want* to.

It's freedom. That's what we kept circling back to. Not just freedom from work but from pressure. From hustle. From the constant triage that parenting demanded. It's a kind of spaciousness we haven't had since before we knew what it cost.

And maybe, if we're lucky, it ends with a martini. Or a movie. Or a text from a kid who suddenly has five free minutes between plans and thinks to call.

We don't know if we'll go two-stepping. Or organize the closets. Or make it to the Maldives before it disappears. But we do know this:

It's not the answers that matter.

It's having someone who still wants to ask the questions with you.

22

Home Alone

Clancy

Okay, so here's the thing: I thought I would love it. The house. Quiet. Just me. No kids. No husband. No one asking what's for dinner or if we're out of laundry detergent. No ESPN in the background. No "Did you already feed the cat?" conversations. I had imagined this little pocket of time as a kind of spa retreat, minus the robe and cucumber water.

And for the first 24 hours, it kind of was.

Rick had gone to Austin for a work trip with a side of family visit, which is his usual rhythm these days. But this time, it hit different. It was the first time since we officially became empty nesters that he had been gone for *days*. Not a quick day trip. Not a "we're both out of town" kind of thing. Just me. In the house. Alone. No kids popping in after school. No husband crashing through the front door with conference calls still ringing in his ears.

Just me. And the cat. (Who, for the record, only appears when there are two voices in the house. One voice? He's out. Zero interest. But if he hears a conversation? Suddenly, he's got opinions.)

I tried to act casual about it. You know, "Oh, this will be good for me. I'll get things done. I'll recharge. Maybe I'll even do a little yoga." (Spoiler: I did not do yoga.)

What I *did* do was pre-fill my calendar like a person afraid of her own company. Life group on Tuesday. Cheer Mom dinner on Wednesday. Every night accounted for, like I was hosting a conference for one. And honestly, I was glad I did. Because while everyone loves alone time in theory, it turns out there's a fine line between solitude and sad-Thursday-night-in-your-pajamas-at-6:00-p.m. energy.

At night, I would call the cat into bed. He's usually banned from sleeping with us—Rick's rules. But with Rick gone, I figured it was Miso's time to shine. Except he wouldn't jump in until the lights were off. As if he knew the rules, and knew I was breaking them, and was just waiting for the plausible deniability of darkness.

It's funny, though. I used to fantasize about this, about space. Mental space. Physical space. Having the TV remote to myself. Not needing to sync schedules or split a frozen pizza. And I got that. For two whole nights.

And then, I missed him.

I missed the banter. The updates from the road. The low-stakes commentary on whatever we were watching on Netflix. The fact that when two voices are in the house, even the cat feels like staying a while.

Maybe that's the sneaky thing about this phase. We think it's about finally getting some peace and quiet. But peace starts to feel weird without someone to share it with.

And, okay, yes, I survived. I didn't burn the house down. Nothing broke. No one had to call a plumber or a neighbor. But when Rick came back, we had a very glamorous date night, and it felt like a kind of homecoming. Like we were reminding ourselves, *Oh yeah, this is what it's like when we make an effort. When we choose to show up. When we're not just sharing a house but a life.*

So yeah, it turns out, I can handle "home alone."

But I like it better when we're home together.

23

We Should Be in Bed by Now

We knew we were too old for this somewhere between stop number three and the second wristband.

Technically, we knew it before that, when we landed in Arizona, hit the grocery store like homing pigeons, and tried to rally for what would become a four-stop night with our son and his friends. But the game had already started. The unspoken dare. The adult-child version of chicken. No one wanted to be the first to say, "Let's call it." So we didn't.

Because here's the thing about visiting your adult kids in college: It's no longer about parent-teacher conferences and cafeteria pizza. It's clubs with cherry blossom walls, sushi that glows under LED light-ing, and a DJ who starts *after* your typical bedtime. It's wristbands. (Wristbands, as if our knees weren't proof enough that we don't belong.)

But we were in. All the way in. Not just physi-cally, though our bodies would pay the price later, but emotionally, too. We wanted to be there. Not in a "trying to be cool" kind of way, but in a "we've got one night, and we're still invited" kind of way.

Rick: I told you I'd go back to Bang Bang.

Clancy: And I was surprised, honestly. I figured you'd tap out after the sushi.

Rick: Oh, I was done. But the pride of staying vertical won out.

We hit Roaring Fork for martinis and memories of Austin. Then Bang Bang, the Japanese-anime-meets-nightclub fever dream that our son had been excited to show us. Then Casey Moore's, where the vibe is low-key and the drinks are green-tea flavored and questionable. Then, somehow, we ended up at a subterranean piano bar called Low Key, belting out "We Are Young" at full volume with college kids who weren't even alive when it came out.

Rick was singing "We Are Old."

Clancy's voice was gone by midnight.

We laughed harder than we expected to. We drank something called a fishbowl and pretended it wasn't terrifying. We watched our son flow from group to group like a natural host, introducing us to his world with pride and ease.

And somewhere in all of that, we remembered a version of ourselves we hadn't hung out with in a while—the fun ones. The say-yes ones. The couple who used to stay out too late and then order tortillas and queso at 2:00 a.m. Only this time, orthotic inserts were involved.

We didn't make it to the final stop. Bang Bang turned back into a club at midnight, and that was our cue. We bowed out gracefully (or at least without tripping over the rope line), handed over the wristbands, and left the night to the people it belonged to.

Clancy: Tanner didn't say it, but I think he was relieved. It was time to shift back to college mode.

Rick: We were a fun cameo, not meant for the full feature.

Clancy: Exactly. And honestly, we didn't need to be.

We stumbled into the dark hotel lobby, lights off, nobody at the desk. We had to use the keycard just to get in. It was one of those moments that felt quiet and cinematic, like the credits were rolling on a very specific kind of night we won't get many more of.

And we felt it. That weird blend of exhaustion, delight, and aching calves. The kind of tired that's earned.

We were too old for it. And we'll probably do it again next time.

Because this season, this strange, beautiful one where your kids still want you around not just as parents but as people they enjoy, it's worth staying up for. Even if we should be in bed by now.

24

The Year We Killed
Valentine's Day

We didn't mean to break up with Valentine's Day. It just sort of happened.

Like a lot of things in long relationships, it wasn't a big, dramatic exit. No slammed doors or angry florists. Just one really bad dinner and a mutual, wordless realization that the glittery pink pressure of February 14 was not for us.

It started, innocently enough, at Houston's. A beloved standby from our dating days, right down the street from Rick's apartment, cozy, predictable, dependable. Except not on Valentine's Day. That night, it was a sweaty holding pen for couples trying to prove their love under heat lamps and prix-fixe menus. We stood elbow-to-elbow with 50 other "romantic" hopefuls, silently calculating how long we could hold out before turning on each other. The tea glasses stayed empty. The chicken tenders were nowhere in sight. (Rick will die on this hill: Houston's makes an elite chicken tender.)

By dessert, or the lack thereof, we looked at each other and just knew: never again, not like this.

That was 20-something years ago. And we've been off script ever since.

There was a time when Valentine's Day was a thing for us. Back in the Donna Lewis years, when singing "I Love You Always Forever" to each other in the car was sweet and mortifying in equal measure. Rick would never admit it publicly, but that song is the cotton candy of our early love story. Pure fluff, but oh so fun.

Then came "Air Supply" (Rick's falsetto impression is... passionate) and Celine Dion's seven-minute operatic rollercoaster, "It's All Coming Back to Me Now." That one he resisted until he found out Meat Loaf wrote it. After that, it became a power ballad of poetic credibility. We'd play it on loop, driving around in our gold Maxima, windows down, feeling things deeply. Probably more than the situation warranted.

But the one that stuck: "Endless Love."

Picture it: post-dinner, driving home from Natale's, a now-defunct Italian spot that knew our names and our wine order. The kind of place where the owner's mom sat in the corner doing tarot readings. On Belt Line, with just the right buzz and a shared affection for Lionel and Diana's '80s fashion sense, we sang to each other. Clancy may or may not have pulled out a hairbrush as a mic. (She says she did. Rick conveniently doesn't remember.) That's the thing about the right song at the right time: It makes you feel 17 and timeless, all at once.

Even now, we just have to look at each other and go, "Bum bum bum bum…" and we're right back there.

Over the years, Valentine's Day drifted from romance to glitter glue.

Clancy became room mom: frog-shaped Valentine boxes, handmade cards, Walmart plushies the size of toddlers. Rick became a Daddy-Daughter Dance regular: tie straight, hair brushed, tiny corsage in hand. The events were sweet, sentimental, and exactly the kind of love that felt real. One year, they went out to dinner with friends before the dance, then slow-danced to "Butterfly Kisses." Cue the collective sigh.

We weren't bitter about losing couple time; we were busy making magic for the kids. And weirdly, that felt just as meaningful.

There were also occasional soccer games. Nothing says romance like bleachers and a concession stand Valentine's dinner. But when you've already opted out of the commercial script, it doesn't feel like a loss. It feels like life.

Of course, there were still gestures. The Spotify mixtape Rick made one year was a modern-day love letter, complete with all our ridiculous and heartfelt favorites. And yes, there were flowers. Not often. Not always on the day. But real ones. Not grocery store guilt bouquets grabbed in the Kroger parking lot. (Though Rick will argue that just because they're from Kroger doesn't mean they aren't fresh.)

To be fair, we had some communication breakdowns early on. Like when Clancy said, "Don't get me flowers; they just die," and Rick, being literal, decided that meant she never wanted flowers again. It took years to undo that programming. Somewhere along the way, she said, "You know, I'd like flowers sometimes," and his brain short-circuited.

Valentine's Day is weird like that. High expectations. Bad intel. A calendar date telling you to feel something on cue.

Then came Arizona.

Technically, we were tagging along on a college visit. Tanner had an honors college tour at ASU, and we figured, hey, if someone else is footing the bill, why not turn it into a getaway?

We dropped him off, then checked into a Scottsdale resort. The sun was shining. The pool was warm. Dinner was casual. No reservations, no crowds, no stress. And just like that, we were back to being a couple on Valentine's Day, not because we were supposed to be but because we wanted to be.

We lay by the pool, ate in the hotel restaurant, and soaked up the ridiculous February perfection of

Arizona. That weekend, we remembered something important: Sometimes, the best way to fall back in love with each other is to do nothing. Together.

So, no, we don't "do" Valentine's Day.

At least, not in the traditional sense. No $300 dinners or mandatory jewelry. No competitive couple selfies. No heart-shaped anything, unless it's on a mixtape or in a kid's craft box.

But we do laugh. And sing. And pour a glass of wine. And sometimes we say, "Remember Natale's?" and then hum that Lionel Richie line and grin at each other like idiots.

25

Hold My Beer, Said the Memory Care

Rick

When you are caring for a parent with dementia, eventually, the surreal becomes familiar. And sometimes, the familiar becomes downright funny—if you let it.

There we were, just planning to visit my mom, maybe grab some coffee, and get back before dark. No big expectations. And then the memory care facility basically said, "Hold my beer." And that's when things got weird, in the best possible way.

Let me rewind.

We make this trip to Austin once a month. My mom's in memory care there. Late-stage Alzheimer's. She's been there for nearly two years now, and if I'm being honest, the beginning of this journey was uncomfortable. I didn't know how to be with her in this new version of herself. I didn't know how to show up.

But now I do, not perfectly, but at least routinely. And this time? This time was something else.

We landed early (thank you, Southwest) and found ourselves with time to kill before visiting hours. It was freezing outside. I mean, Texas-freezing, but still. So we did what any cold, nostalgic couple would do: We went to Kerbey Lane.

The original one. On actual Kerbey Lane.

Clancy looked at me and said, "Last time we were here, we were hungover."

I didn't remember that. She did. She even pointed out the exact table, which probably tells you everything you need to know about how differently we process memories—and tequila.

After breakfast and a stop for coffee beans (because Anderson's Coffee is just that awesome), we headed to see my mom.

The thing about visiting memory care is you don't plan an agenda. You just show up and witness. Sometimes, she's awake. Sometimes, she's not. Sometimes, she knows me. Most times, she doesn't.

That day, she slept through most of our visit. But the place itself was unusually alive. A resident was doing laps around the main hall, as if she were training for a marathon. Every few minutes, she'd stop by, ask if we were doing okay, and offer to get us something. I'm pretty sure she was once a waitress or a concierge. You could tell. The muscle memory of hospitality was still there, even if the context wasn't.

And that's when the absurd started to bloom. Clancy leaned over and whispered, "This is like a frat house."

She wasn't wrong.

There's something about the place—the roaming characters, the guy who regularly shows up with just one shoe and zero explanation, the woman who once dropped her pants in the common area—that feels like a memory care version of a college dorm. But instead of red Solo cups and music blasting from the next room, you've got Bingo schedules and someone loudly insisting it's their turn on the fake fireplace remote.

And it's weirdly wonderful.

I need to pause here and say this: We're not making fun. Alzheimer's is not funny. Watching your mother disappear in slow motion is not funny. But life doesn't pause for grief. And if you don't let yourself laugh, you'll get buried in the weight of it. Humor doesn't erase the ache. It lets you carry it a little longer.

The day only got weirder.

We left the care facility and went to visit my grandmother. She's 99. And she still has the story-telling fire of a camp counselor on night four. Out of nowhere, she told us that when she was a teenager, a fortune teller at a county fair told her she would cross the ocean many times with her children.

Now, remember, this was Quitman, Texas, in the 1940s. People didn't cross oceans unless they were in the Navy or fleeing something. And yet, that's exactly what she did. She raised her family overseas. Lived in France. Visited Germany. They became a family that hopped oceans like puddles.

I'm 50. And I had never heard that story before.

That moment hit me harder than I expected. It reminded me why we show up. Because stories like that, if we don't catch them, disappear forever. They're not archived in some family Google Drive. They live in the folds of memory, passed down, if you're lucky, in a porch conversation with a 99-year-old who still loves it when I bring her baked potato soup.

Later that day, we went back to the care home for my mom's birthday. We expected a small gathering like last year. Family, cake, a few photos.

Instead, we walked into a full production.

Rows of chairs. Decorations. A pianist. It was like a cross between a community theater opening night and the world's most wholesome rave.

Clancy got recruited to pass out cake. She ended up feeding one of the residents, and when I walked over to check in, the woman looked at me, dead serious, and said, "Do you know that man?"

I'm still not sure if she was trying to protect Clancy or flirting with me, maybe both.

At one point, a man sat down wrong on his walker and tumbled backward. Someone shouted, "Cut him off!" as if he were a college kid at his first kegger. And then, not five minutes later, the same man yelled at the punch-pouring staff, "Hey! Keep the drinks coming, lady!"

It was chaos. And joy.

And in the middle of all that noise, my mom, who hadn't spoken three coherent words in weeks, looked up, and when I leaned in and teased her about her "wild party," she smiled and said, "Yeah."

Just one word.

But sometimes one word is everything.

I don't know how much she understands. I don't know what gets through. But I know that day, something did. Maybe it was the music. Maybe it was Nana who held her hand the whole time. Maybe it was just that the room was filled with people who loved her, even if she couldn't name them anymore.

And for once, I didn't think about what we were losing. I thought about what we got to keep, at least for that day.

So yeah. The frat house was in full swing. There were dogs barking, punch bowls tipping, and residents cracking jokes that didn't make sense but somehow made perfect sense. And my mom was in the middle of it, present in her own way.

That's the trick, I think. To meet people where they are. Not where we wish they'd be. To find the beauty in the absurd. The memory in the forgetting.

And maybe, just maybe, to let the chaos be the connection.

26

The Kid Glue

We made it through furniture shopping without a fight. Clothes shopping, too. Back-to-back. That's basically our version of a trust fall.

(And no, it wasn't IKEA. We're not thrill seekers.)

There was a moment, somewhere between arguing over throw pillows and getting lost in the fitting room vortex, where it hit us: This could've gone differently. This whole stage of life, the empty nest, the shift. It could've pulled us apart instead of tightening the knot. It does for many people. And not in a dramatic, movie-montage way. More like a slow dissolve or a quiet unraveling.

We didn't know the term *gray divorce* until recently. (Clancy stumbled across it while Googling "divorce empty nest," which, just to be clear, was for research purposes.)

Apparently, "silver splitters" is a thing, which sounds more like an over-50s jazzercise troupe than a demographic trend, but here we are.

We were listening to a sermon one Sunday—yes, church *and* Google were involved in this one—and the pastor put up a graph. Marital satisfaction over time. And wouldn't you know it? It starts high in the pre-kid days, tanks during preschool (accurate), then flatlines for a bit before curving back upward post-empty nest.

But that curve only rises *if you stick it out.*

Stick it out through the messy middles. Through the years when the only thing you have in common is a shared Google calendar and a mutual hatred of themed science projects. Through the phases when you're not even fighting, you're just roommates who happen to raise the same kids.

We've been there. Our low point hit when our oldest was five. We weren't throwing around the D-word, but we were definitely quiet. Not in the peaceful way. In the way that makes you realize you're living parallel lives under one roof. We took a trip and tried to shake the dust off. Travel became our reset button. (It still is.)

But it wasn't just the vacations. It was the intentional stuff in between. The date nights. The checking in. The "what do you see for us in ten years?"

questions, usually posed by Rick at anniversary dinners while Clancy was just trying to enjoy her pasta. (And now, she's grateful, even if she rolled her eyes at the time.)

The truth is that the empty nest doesn't fix anything. It reveals it. Once the noise dies down—the sports, the school forms, the friend group text threads—you're left with each other. And if that space between you has grown too wide, it doesn't matter how quiet the house is. It's loud.

We've talked about this idea of *Kid Glue*. It's all the things that used to bind us together: the shared logistics, the emergency room visits, the late-night math homework rescues. Even the hard parts created a kind of rhythm. But once that glue's gone, you see the cracks. Or the strength. Or sometimes both.

The stats don't lie. Divorce rates for couples over 50 have doubled since the '90s. Tripled over 65. And it's not just about drifting apart; it's years of slow erosion. Marital neglect. Diverging paths. Even resentment, especially if one person is still clocking in at a full-time job while the other is bingeing Bravo and reorganizing the pantry.

And then there's identity. When you've spent two decades being "so-and-so's mom" or "the soccer dad," what happens when there's no more snack duty? Clancy grieved the laundry, the grocery lists, and the noise. Rick missed his sports buddies and his video game opponents. (They took the Nintendo Switch with them. Rude.)

There's also the other stuff: the aging bodies, the shifting hormones, the gravity. Let's just say that attraction evolves. Or it should. That was part of a conversation we had, and yes, we've had the awkward ones. Clancy once (lovingly) told Rick he was getting soft. Not metaphorically. Physically.

We laugh, but there's truth underneath. Loving someone for a lifetime means loving them as they change and changing with them, not just in theory but in practice. In the way you listen. Touch. Show up. Move your body. Move the furniture. Dream together.

We're not marriage experts. We're just two people who've kept trying. Sometimes awkwardly. Sometimes beautifully. Sometimes with a lot of sarcasm. And definitely with some therapy along the way.

PART III

Spring

27

Spring Break, Remixed

Clancy

Okay, I thought I'd be fine. I mean, we've done the whole come-home-for-break-then-go-back-to-college thing before. We're in the rhythm now. You hug, you wave, you toss in a "text me when you land," and then you move on with your Sunday.

Except this time, I didn't.

This time, I watched Teagan roll her little carry-on toward the security line, and I felt that weird, tight-squeezed sadness in my chest. That ache that shows up when you didn't realize you were going to miss someone *that* much *that* fast.

Teagan had decided not to wrangle a spring break trip with friends, so we planned one together, just the three of us. It was spontaneous, easy, and somehow exactly what we all needed. We walked New York City until our feet gave out, ate more carbs than is nutritionally advised, and went to back-to-back Broadway shows like we were 22 and flush with time. And in all of that, I wasn't "Mom" the whole time. I mean, I was, but I also wasn't. I was her travel buddy. Her museum sidekick. Her "split the cheesecake" partner at 10:00 p.m. in a tiny pub where we probably over-tipped because we were just so happy.

The trip brought me face-to-face with the reality of parenting in this phase. Like, Teagan was the one holding the map at the museum. She was the one spouting off facts about rocks and fossils, and I was the one following her around, going, "Wait, how do you know that?" (Answer: Her classes. Apparently, tuition *is* doing something.)

And yes, I still did her laundry the night before she flew back because old habits die hard. But I also got to walk beside her on the High Line and see the world through her eyes: funny, observant, wide open. And let me tell you, when your college kid is the one organizing the subway routes and suggesting food tours, you both start to realize something: You're not steering the ship anymore. And that's weird, but also kind of wonderful.

One of the most memorable moments was this build-your-own Reese's thing across from our hotel. Teagan had seen it on Instagram (of course, she had) and said, "I really want to do that." Which, okay, I was expecting maybe a fun-size candy. But no. This thing was the size of her head, like, literally. A full pound of peanut butter with mix-ins and chocolate poured over the top like it was some kind of candy volcano. And I just stood there laughing, watching her face light up like she was eight again and I'd just surprised her with a new plushie.

It was ridiculous and fun and a little too much, just like her, in the best way.

That night, we saw *Six*, her favorite musical. She'd seen it before. Twice. Once all alone, pre-COVID, last-minute ticket, she sat by herself like a tiny theater-loving adult. I remember thinking at the time, *Should we let her go alone?* But now, that girl could probably direct the show. She knew every beat, every harmony. She was glowing.

Later, when she was gone and the house felt too quiet again, Rick said, "I didn't feel sad this time because it felt full. Nothing was missing."

And he's right. That's what this trip gave us. Not just a break but a *remix*. A reintroduction to who we are now and who our kids are becoming. You spend so many years parenting from a place of keeping them alive, on schedule, and somewhat decent to other humans. But now? Now we get to know them again. As grown-ups. As people. And if you're lucky, as friends.

So yeah, I cried a little when she left.

But I also felt so damn proud. Of her. Of us. Of this weird, wonderful, in-between season where you get to watch your kid book the hotel and navigate the subway and order the ramen and still, somehow, want to split dessert with you at the end of the night.

It's not the dramatic goodbye of that first college drop-off. It's the simple "see you soon" that sneaks up and makes you ache in the best, most hopeful kind of way.

28

That's Life

We'd just come off a full spring break: dinners with Teagan, staying out past our bedtime, and actual plans on multiple nights. The kind of uninterrupted time you miss once your kids grow up and schedules no longer overlap. For a few days, it felt like a rewind button had been pressed. Familiar rhythms. Full tables. Noise.

And then came the drop.

Not a crash, exactly. More like a slow deflation. We returned to a house that felt too quiet, with bodies that were too tired, and a calendar that didn't get the memo that we were done being social. It's strange how something can be good and still be too much.

The post-vacation fog rolled in, bringing with it allergies, minor ailments, and that weird disorientation when the house is both peaceful and, somehow, heavy.

We'd overcommitted ourselves. Again. (We never learn.) Three evening plans in five days—rookie move. Somewhere between drying her hair and locating a second pair of wedges, Clancy mutinied. The body said no before the brain could protest. She swapped her outfit for pajamas and declared the night canceled. Meanwhile, Rick launched into recovery mode via Zelda, noise-canceling headphones, and total avoidance.

Which, honestly, says everything.

This is the dance of marriage in the empty nest: One of us needs quiet connection; the other needs just quiet. Both are valid. Both are necessary. Neither comes with a user manual.

• • •

But somewhere amid that social fatigue, we found ourselves surprised by joy again.

It was just dinner with our new Life Group, six couples crammed around two pushed-together tables, squinting at laminated menus under the glow of overhead lighting that made everyone look vaguely seasick. The server was frazzled, the drinks took forever, and one couple accidentally sat at the wrong restaurant for 20 minutes before realizing they were supposed to be next door.

And yet, somehow, it worked.

We went in thinking it might be awkward. That we'd spend two hours making polite conversation, then politely decline future invitations because making friends as an adult is a minefield, especially without the safety net of sports bleachers, PTA meetings, or chaotic birthday parties to lean on.

But then the table started splitting into rhythms. On one end, the women dove into an intense, wildly speculative discussion about Kate Middleton's disappearance from the public eye. ("No, but seriously, have you *seen* that video?") On the other end, three grown men discovered a shared obsession with FlightAware and suddenly bonded over tail numbers and turbulence, as if they were at an aviation convention. (Rick is still unclear on whether one of them actually owns a small aircraft or just *talks* like he does.)

Clancy gave Rick a look from across the table, the silent one that says, *We might've found our people.*

By the time dessert menus hit the table, we were trading Netflix recs and allergy remedies like old friends. No one tried too hard. No one overshared. And no one needed to pretend they weren't tired by 8:45.

And that, too, is life now. You wade through awkward hellos, hoping to find your people. When you do, it's a gift. When you don't, well, there's still dessert.

● ● ●

Saturday came in wet and sluggish. The kind of day that never really gets started. Rain on the windows, laundry in the dryer, Zelda calling Rick's name from the upstairs TV like some pixelated siren. We were ready for quiet.

Miso had other plans.

He's technically Teagan's cat, but college distance makes that a very loose definition. We are the ones currently on the hook for his grooming, his moods, and his complete refusal to enter a carrier without a scene that rivals a hostage negotiation.

The goal was simple: clip his nails. The strategy? Evolving in real time.

Step one: Calming treats. He sniffed them, batted one off the table, then stared at us like *this is insulting*. Step two: Clancy fell down a YouTube rabbit hole of grooming tutorials that made it look so easy. "Just swaddle your cat gently, as if wrapping a baby." Lies. All of it.

Eventually, we landed on the most basic plan: sneak attack. It was raining, and he was dozing on the upstairs cushion beside Rick, lulled by the gentle drone of side quests and sword clashes from the TV. Clancy entered the room slowly, holding the tube of meat paste like a grenade pin already pulled. Miso perked up, sniffed, intrigued.

Then the blanket came out.

She wrapped him like a burrito, tight but loving. Rick, now sprawled on the floor in full containment mode, dangled the meat goo like bait. ("Hold it closer. No, not that close, he's losing interest. Oh no, he's wiggling. Grab the paw!") We got through two claws, maybe three. And then he exploded backward out of the blanket like a caffeinated raccoon. Gone.

Clancy was face-down on the carpet, cat hair stuck to her lip balm. Rick was still holding the goo tube, now ignored. We just lay there, staring at the ceiling, and started laughing. Because what else do you do?

You think this stage of life will be all dinners out and unplanned road trips. Sometimes, it's playing cat groomer and talking in your serious voice to a feral animal who absolutely doesn't care.

And just when we thought that was the crescendo? Tornado sirens.

Because of course. The sky turned green, the alerts went off, and suddenly we were sprinting into the hall closet while Miso went full panic, diving under Teagan's bed like it was a World War II bunker. Rain turned to hail—loud, fast, punishing. It sounded like the house was being pelted with gravel. We crouched in the dark, wedged between old blankets and a Costco box of Christmas decor, wondering aloud if the cat was okay and if anyone remembered to close the garage door.

• • •

That night, we went to see *Kung Fu Panda 4*. Just the two of us sitting in those reclining chairs with too much legroom, still quoting lines from the original under our breath.

And yet, they were with us.

Teagan had already texted from Arizona to say she was planning to see it that afternoon with her roommate. Tanner had a group outing lined up that night. Without meaning to, the four of us ended up watching it on the same day, from three different states.

That felt like something.

We'd introduced them to the series when they were tiny, back when animated movies weren't a genre; they were a lifestyle. When Tanner couldn't sit still and Teagan needed to be held the whole time. We owned the DVD. The action figures. At least one Po-adorned t-shirt. And now, here we were, all grown up, still laughing at Jack Black's noodle jokes.

Somehow, it felt like a loop quietly closing. Just a quiet little "we made it" whispered from the back row.

That's life, too.

• • •

A few days later, we got a text from a friend. Their family had just said goodbye to their dog of 16 years.

Amanda wrote, "It's so quiet. His fur is still everywhere, but I can't bring myself to vacuum yet."

Because of course it's about the dog, but it's also not. Sixteen years means that dog lived every season of their parenting life. From elementary school drop-offs to high school graduations. From potty training to college tours. That fur, still clinging to couch cushions and corners, wasn't just fur. It was the physical trace of a life stage you can't get back.

We sent Amanda and her family love and prayers because what else is there to say? There are no adequate words for moments like this, when the silence isn't just a missing bark or jingling collar, it's the space left behind by everything that used to fill the house.

You lose a pet, and suddenly you're grieving more than an animal. You're grieving a whole era.

• • •

That week, while we were still recovering from the emotional whiplash of it all, Teagan texted us. She was working on a major sociology project about school violence. Not guns, specifically. Just the lived experience. And as part of it, she was interviewing people who'd been directly affected. She'd already talked to her best friend. Now she wanted to include us.

Because we had been affected. More than once.

The first time was her freshman year of high school, Tanner's senior year. The school went into lockdown over a threat. We remember the day, vaguely. But her questions forced us to go back. "Where were you when you heard?" she asked. We didn't remember exactly. So we scrolled through our old text thread.

And there it was.

"If something happens, I love you guys."

That was from her. Just a freshman in high school, texting her parents because she didn't know how the day would end.

Reading it again, all we could think was, *This isn't the kind of love note any child should have to send.*

• • •

So we grieve. But we also laugh. Because grief alone is too heavy to carry, and joy alone feels like denial. And this stage is learning how to hold both.

That's life.

It's brushing the cat and brushing up against mortality. It's missing your kids and still going to the movie first. It's bourbon one week and herbal tea the next. It's tornado sirens and kung fu pandas. It's grief and pollen and meat goo in a tube.

It's all of it. The mundane. The ridiculous. The hard. The deeply human.

And we're living it the best we know how.

29

Love, Basketball, and a Hole in the Wall

We didn't mean for our marriage to become a timeline of basketball tournaments, but here we are. We can chart our lives by Duke's March Madness schedule: Games at Ben's Half Yard House (dating), the San Antonio regional final (early marriage), the Final Four that got hijacked by our daughter's birth (parenthood), and now, the empty nest, where the games are quieter but somehow sweeter.

Rick will tell you he wasn't even a basketball fan growing up. "We weren't that family," he says, "no season tickets, no tailgating, no yelling at the TV." He remembers stumbling onto a UT game on the radio in high school, staying up past his bedtime to listen. That was the spark. But he'll also tell you (with great indignation) that when he chose Duke, he had no idea it was a basketball school. (Clancy would like it on record: *How is that even possible?*)

By the time the Christian Laettner shot happened his freshman year—*the* shot, the one still played in March Madness montages—he was all in. If you watch ESPN's "I Hate Christian Laettner" 30-for-30 documentary, you can actually see Rick in the background of the crowd, living his best basketball life. (We've paused and pointed him out to the kids. Tanner thought it was so cool; Teagan was, perhaps appropriately, unimpressed.)

Clancy's childhood was the opposite. Sports were everywhere. Her dad filled out newspaper brackets, football games blared in the background, and the family calendar revolved around who was playing when. But she didn't really *care*. "It was just there," she says now. "Background noise. I wasn't invested."

That changed when we started dating. Rick's Duke obsession was contagious. He pulled Clancy into road trips to regional finals in San Antonio, spontaneous TV marathons, and buzzer-beater highs that were impossible not to feel. "Once you're in a packed stadium and everyone's screaming," Clancy says, "you stop being neutral. You pick a side. And Rick's side was Duke."

It wasn't long before she wasn't just along for the ride anymore. She knew the players, she understood the stakes, and she could hold her own in the trash talk. Basketball had moved from background noise to shared language.

That intensity carried into our early years together. We once decided on a whim to drive to San Antonio for a regional final. We had no tickets, no hotel reservation, and no plan. We ended up in a dingy motel somewhere outside the city limits, the kind of place where you sleep in your clothes for "extra protection," but we didn't care. Duke was playing.

By the time we were engaged, basketball had become such a fixture in our lives that we scheduled our wedding around the tournament. "No March weddings," Rick told Clancy, dead serious. "Or the first weekend in April, either." We laugh about it now, but at the time, she was accommodating a man who would one day drill a hole in our living room wall for March Madness.

Yes, a hole. In Houston, pre-WiFi, CBS's regional coverage meant you could easily miss Duke games if you lived in the wrong ZIP code. Rick couldn't risk it. So one night, in a fit of bracket-season engineering, he ran coax cable through a freshly drilled hole between rooms just so he could stream alternate games from the computer onto the TV. This was the dial-up era, mind you, when you had to yell at everyone to get off the phone so you could connect. The picture quality was atrocious, but we didn't care. Duke was on. We never repaired that hole, just shoved a piece of furniture in front and hoped the next homeowners wouldn't notice.

Our kids, of course, were born into this rhythm. Tanner's middle name is Cameron. Rick insists it's just because we liked the name; Clancy maintains Cameron Indoor Stadium, the famously tiny, deafening arena at Duke, where students camp out for weeks just to get inside, was a not-so-subtle influence. And then there's Teagan, who was born on Championship Monday, four weeks early, while Rick stood in the delivery room talking Duke versus Carolina with the doctor. (Clancy, in stirrups: "Hello? I'm having a baby here.")

These days, the obsession has mellowed. We're less likely to center an entire weekend around a game and more likely to watch outdoors with neighbors, a drink in hand, sunlight on our faces. But March Madness still holds this nostalgic weight. Our kids have their own brackets now. Tanner (Arizona State) and Teagan (Arizona) text each other trash talk from opposite ends of the rivalry. We sit in the group thread, quiet observers, popping metaphorical popcorn as their comebacks get saltier.

And this is what we didn't see coming about the empty nest: how much joy there is in the background. We're not the focal point of our kids' lives anymore, and that's okay. Beautiful, even. Their banter—about basketball, about anything—tells us they'll carry each other forward long after we're out of the picture.

So, yes. Basketball is still a big deal in our house. There's still a part of Rick that gets unreasonably cranky when Duke loses. (Clancy once had a *very effective* method for pulling him out of that mood. Let's just say it involved lingerie. That incentive is long gone, and so he sulks.) But even the losses don't sting like they used to.

We've learned something over the years: Life, like the tournament, is full of upsets. You can't plan for every outcome. Sometimes, your daughter shows up four weeks early on the day of the championship. Sometimes, your team misses the Final Four. And sometimes, you just grab an Adirondack chair, watch the game outside, and know that whatever happens on the court, you've already won.

30

Ever Evolving Easter

We used to think Easter meant one thing: being at my parents' house. (Clancy here. Rick would probably add "and wearing pastel-colored shirts that I swore weren't intentional.") The kids knew the rhythm by heart: wake up to Easter baskets, go to church, PopPop hides color-coded eggs in the backyard, ham and mashed potatoes for lunch. That was Easter. We didn't even have to think about it.

But this year, Easter was Arizona. Again.

If you had told us ten years ago that we'd be flying to Tucson on Good Friday with carry-ons stuffed with spring clothes and leftover Reese's eggs, we'd have laughed. Easter was supposed to be anchored in a place, in a house. Instead, here we were shoving our roller bags into the overhead bins, trying not to lose our boarding group, making our way across Denver's airport like we were auditioning for *The Amazing Race*. (We did not win.)

It's a strange shift, this empty nest thing. Holidays used to orbit around us. Now we orbit around the kids.

We landed in Tucson just in time to scoop up Teagan from the gym. She looked happy, really happy. Her first semester had been good, but there was a different lightness about her now. New dorm, new roommate, friends who felt like family. She wanted to go to Target (of course), so we did the Target run, then ducked into Walmart for something we forgot. And there, in the frozen food aisle, we ran into her new roommate. We shook hands, made small talk, and did the parental mental inventory: Does she seem nice? (She did.) Does Teagan seem relaxed? (She did.)

We were absurdly grateful for that accidental run-in. Parenting adult kids is basically one long exercise in gathering clues: Are they okay? Are they thriving? Are they eating actual vegetables? That smile in the Walmart aisle was a clue, and it gave us peace.

Saturday, we drove up to Tempe with Teagan in the back seat. No one complained about the two-hour drive. Honestly, it felt like a gift, just the three of us in the car, no distractions. Tanner was waiting for us, a little groggy from cold medicine. We did the grocery store run (of course), then stopped for sandwiches at a place we like.

And that's when it hit Rick.

"I just need y'all to know," he said at the table, "how lucky we are that we can do this, that we actually want to do this. It's not normal to be able to gather like this so easily."

It was true. As much as we miss the comfort of the old traditions, there was something beautiful about this new version: four people in a sandwich shop in Tempe, laughing about nothing and everything.

That night, we went to Easter service at a Scottsdale church that has basically become "our" Arizona church. (Twice makes it ours, right?) Clancy cried when the kids stood on either side of her during worship. Rick teared up, too, though he tried to play it cool. These days, we find ourselves getting emotional about the simplest things.

After church, we went out for Italian food with Tanner's roommates. The waitress asked if we were celebrating something. "Easter," we said, "and these boys about to graduate." She nodded like she understood. Maybe she did.

We flew home the next day, Easter lunch reduced to Cheez-Its and protein bars from Teagan's campus market (which we, of course, paid for). It was not the Easter of BiBi's ham and Pop Pop's egg hunts. There were no cascarones with confetti that stuck in our hair for days.

But it was good.

Traditions change when your kids leave home. They have to. That used to make us sad, but now it feels hopeful. We'll carry some pieces with us—the color-coordinated pastels, the church service, the big meal—but we're learning that the heart of the holiday isn't the place or the menu.

It's being together, even if "together" now means airports, hotel rooms, and an Easter service in a city we don't live in.

We'll figure out next year when it comes. Maybe we'll be back at BiBi and Pop Pop's. Maybe we'll be somewhere completely new. We just know we'll find a way to gather, even if it looks different from how it used to.

31

A Map of Our Marriage in Four Houses

We didn't mean to create a roadmap of our marriage out of floor plans, but here we are, four houses later, able to chart the entire arc of our life together in square footage and backyard trees.

Our first house was in Dallas, a 1940s bungalow on the M Streets that looked charming and was held together mostly by sheer willpower (and a lot of tulip bulbs). We bought it a few months before we got married, which meant we learned how to be homeowners before we'd figured out how to be husband

and wife. Squirrels in the attic. A cracked window we didn't notice for months. A neighbor literally asking if she could dig up all the lilies in our yard. We didn't have a clue, but we had a dog named Kibo and a backyard that felt like freedom. Looking back, we were so young that we made inflatable kiddie pools look like an intentional design choice.

A year later, we packed it all up and moved to Houston. Rick had taken a job there, and we were in that stage of life where "why not?" was our default answer. That house was a one-story ranch with an enormous backyard and no sprinkler system. We learned how to drag hoses around every inch of that lawn while also learning how to care for a newborn, because this was the house we brought Tanner home to. Our neighbors were kind, the margarita machine was a fixture at birthday parties, and the fence we installed ourselves probably would've fallen over in a stiff wind. But it was ours.

By the time we moved to Flower Mound, life was moving faster. Clancy was seven months pregnant with Teagan, Tanner was just shy of three, and we bought the house during a snowstorm, which is not how we recommend making major life decisions. The house itself never really felt like "the one." The layout was odd, and the neighborhood was still developing. But the memories are woven into its walls: Tanner bouncing on the couch singing U2's *Vertigo*, Teagan pressing her tiny hands against the window, desperate to follow her big brother outside. It's where we learned that fasting together is a surefire way to start a fight, and that kids will climb literally any-thing, including your leg, if it gets them closer to strawberries.

And then there's this house, the one we've been in for 17 years. Our Frisco home, the so-called "for-ever house" we built when Tanner was heading into kindergarten and Teagan was about to turn two. We pulled the grill out front the first week we moved in and met every neighbor on the street. The kids grew up like stair steps with the other kids who moved in at the same time. We've hosted graduation parties, weddings, and too many poolside summer nights to count. There's a tree in the front yard that was once uprooted in a storm and somehow survived. It now towers over the house like it's always been there.

We've been here so long that Rick will soon have lived in this house longer than he lived in his child-hood home. That's a strange thought. What does it mean when the house that raised your kids also raised you?

Sometimes, we talk about moving now. The wind in North Texas is brutal, and the kids are grown. Nothing is tying us to this exact address anymore. And yet, we know that leaving will be complicated. This house has been the backdrop of our family's greatest joys and hardest seasons. It's where we've been Rick-and-Clancy-the-parents for nearly two decades.

But here's what we've learned from every move: The house is never really the thing. The thing is the life lived inside of it. Each home felt irreplaceable at the time, and then we packed up and started over. We'll do it again someday.

When we drove through our old neighborhoods recently, we couldn't help but point and say, "Remember that house?" Like landmarks on a map, each one held a piece of our story. The walls didn't remember us, but we remembered them. And maybe that's the quiet magic of this stage of life: realizing the places we've called home were never meant to hold us forever.

32

Cakes on a Plane

Clancy

In case you've ever wondered, frosting is technically a "spreadable," which means it's a liquid, so TSA can and will confiscate it. I know this now because I had to Google it at 10:00 p.m. the night before flying with my daughter's 19th birthday cake.

This was the first birthday Teagan wasn't going to spend at home, and it turns out, I wasn't remotely ready to let that tradition go. I've made the same strawberry cake for her since she was six, always in the shape of the year she's turning. It's not even that complicated of a cake, but it's our thing, and she loves it. And this year, apparently, I was determined to hand-carry it 900 miles to Arizona.

Rick (deadpan, from the kitchen): "You know you could just buy a cake when we get there, right?"

Sure. I could. But it wouldn't be *the* cake.

Which is how I ended up walking through Dallas Love Field Airport with a cake carrier tucked under my arm like it was a priceless artifact. TSA didn't even blink (for the record, frosted cakes are fine; unfrosted cakes with a tub of icing are not). But fellow travelers did. By the time we connected through Denver, people were literally pointing. One dad even leaned down to his toddler and said, "Are you looking at that cake?"

I'm not going to lie, it felt like a bit of a mom-rockstar moment.

What Teagan didn't know was that the cake was coming. She knew we'd show up for dinner, but the cake, well, that's where traditions matter. When I finally pulled it out of the front seat of the rental car, buckled in with its own seatbelt, she gasped. She was shocked. I think she might have cried a little, though she'd deny it because her friends were there.

I didn't need the tears. That tiny intake of breath was enough to know that she felt loved.

• • •

Rick

Less than 24 hours later, we were in a completely different kind of audience, this time sitting in the back of a small Honors College classroom, watching Tanner defend his senior thesis.

Now, I knew this would be a serious thing. But I didn't realize it would feel like the academic version of a courtroom drama. Two professors on one side of the table, Tanner on the other, fielding questions about Japan's 99.8% conviction rate like his diploma depended on it. (Which, as it turns out, it kind of did.)

Clancy kept whispering, "I feel like I'm back in school," which only confirmed what I was already thinking: We were completely useless here. There was no raising a hand to clarify, no slipping him an answer from the sidelines. We were just observers.

Parenthood ends in stages, and this was one of those moments I could feel it happening in real time. Tanner didn't need us to step in. He didn't even need us to nod reassuringly. He had it handled.

Of course, I couldn't help but notice the tiny things: how he leaned into the questions instead of dodging them, how he slipped in a joke at exactly the right moment, how one professor tried to poke holes in his argument, and he calmly patched them without flinching.

When they finally sent us all out into the hallway to "deliberate," I realized I'd been holding my breath for a solid hour.

And then came the verdict: "Congratulations. You've successfully defended, with revisions."

I almost laughed out loud. Of course, there were revisions. There are always revisions. But Tanner? He just smiled, shook their hands, and walked out like the weight of a year-long project had just slid off his shoulders.

That's the moment it hit me: We weren't the ones holding him up anymore. We were just the ones in the back row, grinning like fools, proud beyond measure.

• • •

Clancy

On the flight home, I kept thinking about the sheer effort of it all: the cake, the cross-country travel, the logistics, and the expense. Are we just filling our calendar with trips to the kids, so we don't have to sit in the quiet house?

Maybe.

But here's the thing: Some of that effort is just how we love. It's how we tell our kids, "We're here, even if it's a little crazy, even if you don't technically need us."

Teagan said something to me as I was helping carry her birthday gifts back to her dorm: "I have great parents."

That one little sentence undid me.

Because the truth is, the house will still be quiet. And yes, there will be a day when there's no cake to carry and no thesis to sit through. But for now, we'll take the travel, the early flights, and the tiny moments that feel bigger than they look.

Rick: Even if it means packing another ridiculous cake onto a plane.

Clancy: Don't tempt me.

33

We've Been There

We were just leaving Ozona when we saw them. A mom, a dad, a little girl in a glittery competitive cheer uniform, and two boys—identical twins, if we had to guess—around YMCA soccer age. One of the boys was in full meltdown mode. The kind where he goes rigid as a board in the parking lot, and the parents have to decide whether to carry him in like a sack of potatoes or just pretend they don't know him.

We froze like we were watching a nature documentary. *Ah, yes, the American suburban family in its natural habitat: post-cheer-competition, pre-meal, navigating one child's volcanic eruption while desperately craving queso and a beer.*

The dad looked like he'd been trapped at a cheer comp all day and was now singularly focused on watching the Masters. The mom had the "I just want to sit down and not be touched" face. Neither of them wanted to go home. But the little boy was not having it.

And then she said it. The line every parent has uttered at least once in their life:

"I am not having this."

We watched as she turned the entire family around and marched them back to the car. The boy, now realizing that his protest had backfired, began wailing even louder.

We got in our car and just sat there for a second. And then we looked at each other.

Clancy: "Oh my gosh, that was us. That was *exactly* us."

Rick: "Cheer and soccer Saturdays. I think I still have orange slices in my car from 2009."

Clancy: "Remember that one time Tanner threw up in the Chick-fil-A drive-thru after practice?"

Rick: "Which time?"

There was a time when this was our life: loading kids into car seats, hauling gear bags, missing nap windows, trying to hold onto our sanity with snack bribes. We wouldn't trade those years for anything, but there's something delicious about being able to go out for lunch on a whim without anyone screaming because we forced them to order something other than chicken nuggets at our favorite Mexican restaurant.

The freedom of the empty nest isn't about extravagant trips or reinventing yourself overnight. Sometimes, it's just the ability to linger over lunch and watch a young family struggle, knowing you survived that season and that it does, in fact, get easier.

We didn't say anything to them. (You can't, really. No parent wants unsolicited wisdom in the middle of a parking lot meltdown.) But in our heads, we whispered what we wish someone had told us back then:

You're doing great. It won't always be this hard. One day, you'll walk out of a restaurant at noon and realize you have no schedule at all. And you'll sit in your car and savor it.

And maybe watch other families melt down just a little too long—out of solidarity, of course.

34

Unicorns and Trolls

We'll admit it; we sort of expected the empty nest to feel lighter. And in many ways, it does. There are date nights that don't start with, "What time do we need to be back?" There's spontaneous travel, less laundry, and fewer shoes in the hallway. We have closet space again (largely because Clancy has taken over Tanner's closet).

But it's not all rainbows and unicorns when the kids leave. Sure, there are plenty of both, moments of pure wonder and freedom, but there are trolls under the bridge, too.

We felt it just last week. We'd spent the day visiting Rick's mom, who's living with Alzheimer's, and it left us quiet on the drive home. Seeing someone you love slip further into the fog is a kind of heartbreak you can't tidy up with gratitude. We tried. We reminded ourselves we're lucky to see her, lucky she's in good hands. But the reality is, when you see the glimmers of who she used to be, then watch them fade again, it wears on you.

Then there's work. Rick's job has been, well, let's just say the unicorns aren't exactly galloping through the office. It's one of those seasons where you're doing all the right things, but the results aren't there. Powerlessness has a way of sneaking in through multiple doors at once: aging parents, uncertain careers, even the never-ending to-do list that waits at home.

And yet.

In the same week, we got a text from one of the kids sharing a small victory at school. We laughed with Rick's sister over ridiculous family stories while making dinner. We had a glass of wine on the patio and noticed how the spring light hit the trees in the backyard. That's the strange thing about this phase of life: The trolls don't cancel out the unicorns, and the unicorns don't banish the trolls. They just coexist.

We've learned to stop pretending it's supposed to be one or the other. We can be grateful and gutted at the same time. We can feel lucky and still let it suck. We can sit in the car after visiting his mom, cry, then go home and laugh at a meme the kids sent us.

Maybe that's the real magic trick of the empty nest: learning to hold it all without rushing to make it neat. Let the trolls be there under the bridge. They're part of the landscape. But so are the unicorns. And every so often, when the rainbows show up, you just stand there and let yourself feel the light.

35

Conversations We'd Rather Not Have

Clancy

We didn't plan for a Saturday afternoon to end in estate planning. But there we were, sitting around my parents' dining room table with my brother, a neat stack of labeled folders, and enough unspoken tension in the air to make me wish for an actual escape hatch.

This is what happens in the empty nest. One day, you're trying to figure out what to do with all the leftover soccer trophies in the attic, and the next, you're helping your parents decide who gets the sideboard in the living room if—no, when—they're gone. It's the kind of conversation no one wants to have, but avoiding it doesn't make it go away.

I'm the middle child, the daughter, the peacemaker. And as we talked through my parents' plans—wills, powers of attorney, passwords—my childhood role resurfaced, as if it had been waiting for its cue. My dad and older brother started to edge toward one of their familiar debates, voices rising a little too much, and there I was again: "Okay, let's settle that later. We don't need to go down that path right now." (Middle children everywhere, I see you.)

Rick leaned on what he calls his "business brain," the part of him that can turn any emotionally charged situation into a bullet-point list. "Start with the shared objective," he reminded us later. It sounds corporate, but it works. If everyone agrees, "We want Mom and Dad to be cared for, and we want the family to stay connected," then you can come back to that when the conversations get hard or awkward.

And they do get awkward. Even in our families, where we're lucky to have close relationships and positive intent, the process is uncomfortable. You feel the role reversal pressing on you: You're no longer looking to the generation above you for guidance. You're guiding them forward. That's a heavy shift.

We've seen what happens when families avoid these conversations. Rick lost his dad unexpectedly at 57, when Tanner was barely a year old, and he remembers the blur of having to make decisions he wasn't ready to make. "There's no playbook for that," he said, "but I know now how much pain could have been eased if we'd had those talks ahead of time."

So now we lean in, even when it feels like we're prying. We ask the questions we don't want to ask: Where are the important documents? Who has access to the bank accounts? Which mattress might have the "hidden pearls" in it?

It's not just about logistics. It's about giving everyone the chance to grieve without chaos. It's about preserving relationships when stress is highest. And honestly, it's about relief—relief that we won't be scrambling later, trying to decode what Mom and Dad "would have wanted" while also trying to keep the lights on and the water bill paid.

We left that day with a few gaps to close, but mostly with gratitude. Gratitude for parents willing to have the hard conversations. Gratitude for siblings who, even when we rib each other, show up. Gratitude for the space this empty nest season gives us to tackle the things we kept pushing off when the kids were small and we were just trying to keep everyone fed.

If you're in this stage, here's our unsolicited advice: Have the conversations now. Yes, they'll be awkward. Yes, someone will probably roll their eyes. But one day you'll be thankful you did, and so will the people you love.

36

We Used Up All Our Words

We don't remember who said it first, probably Tanner, but by the end of graduation week, it was the only sentence any of us could manage: "I think we've used up all our words."

And we had. Days of ceremonies, parties, dinners, and photo ops had wrung us out like damp towels. We'd clapped until our hands hurt, smiled until our cheeks ached, and told Tanner "Congratulations!" at least 4,000 times. By the time we were sitting in a booth at Sunny's Diner that final morning, we were beyond words. Just four people poking at pancakes, occasionally making eye contact like, "Still alive? Great."

The week was a blur in the best way. We'd changed our flight to arrive early (because nothing says "party parents" like landing just in time for a bar crawl) and somehow ended up beating Tanner and his friends to the first stop. There we were, two parents holding adult beverages at a college bar on Mill Avenue at 11:00 a.m., getting waved in by his friends like we actually belonged there.

Rick, who would like it noted for the record, actually started the bar crawl at 42,000 feet, thanks to an 8:00 a.m. Wild Turkey on the flight in. He even sent a picture of it to Tanner mid-air, as if to say, "We're already cooler than your friends."

The celebrations rolled from there: ceremonies in football stadiums and honors halls, late-night family dinners at restaurants that doubled as clubs (because why not add thumping bass to your sushi order?), and dozens of small moments that somehow felt bigger than the official events.

We watched Tanner walk across stage after stage, each time wondering, *How is this already the end?* He was no longer an ASU student; he was just a random guy in Tempe now. We knew he'd stay for the summer, and the thought of him being there without the cushion of classes and roommates made us both feel protective and nostalgic. Rick remembered his post-graduation summer—quiet dorms, empty streets—and knew how disorienting it could be.

But even as the ceremonies blurred together, other things stood out sharply.

Like the first ride we took in a Waymo, a driverless car that felt more sci-fi than suburban-parent-approved. We loved it so much we insisted on sending Teagan in one, certain that she'd be safer in a car without a driver than with some random Uber guy. (Nothing against Uber guys, just, you get it.)

Or the family dinner at Pasta Brioni, the same little Italian place we'd discovered on Tanner's first Parents' Weekend four years ago. It felt right to be there again on the other side of it all, twirling the same pasta, raising the same glasses, closing the circle.

And then there was the phone call about Rick's mom. We'd known it was coming—Alzheimer's had been slowly taking her from us for years—but the timing was brutal. The day of the main graduation ceremonies, we got word that she was likely to pass within hours. She died the next day.

We told the kids what was happening that morning, but we didn't stop the celebrations. We knew she wouldn't have wanted that. So we kept going—laughing, hugging, eating, posing for pictures—while carrying a quiet layer of grief in the background. That's midlife in a nutshell, isn't it? Joy and loss, pride and heartbreak, all braided together so tightly you can't tell where one ends and the other begins.

By the last night, we were emotionally and physically toast. We'd Waymoed and walked, clapped and toasted, hugged and said goodbye a dozen different ways. The boys' graduation robes smelled like a frat house. Tanner asked if we'd come pick up the stuff he'd left at a bar at midnight, and we were already in pajamas. (Answer: Absolutely not.)

We ended the week the way we'd started it: together, tired, and a little teary. And somewhere between the last bite of diner pancakes and the drive to the airport, we realized that the quiet we were returning to would sound louder than ever.

Because graduation doesn't just mark the end of a school year, it marks the end of an era.

And this time, it wasn't just Tanner who was stepping into a new chapter.

PART IV

Summer

37

Empty Nest, Full House (Again)

We were just starting to find our rhythm again. Empty nest life had this quiet but lively hum to it: morning coffee without interruption, spontaneous happy hours, and actual control over the thermostat. We'd gotten used to walking through a house that stayed exactly the way we left it. The fridge wasn't mysteriously empty, our schedules weren't tied to anyone else's comings and goings, and our evenings were ours alone.

And then, without warning, the hum turned into a full-blown marching band the moment Teagan walked through the door for the summer.

We love having her home, truly. But the shift is instant. One minute, it's the two of us debating where to go for dinner; the next, it's, "Mom, we need a Target run," and "Dad, can we squeeze in ramen before my shift?" Our bedroom, which had become this serene sanctuary, was once again the gathering spot for late-night catchups, Miso the cat weaving figure eights around us like he'd been waiting for his pack to reunite.

The first night she was back, Clancy and Teagan set up on the couch for a *Trolls* marathon. It wasn't exactly Clancy's idea of cinematic art, but when your daughter pulls you into her world, complete with gummy worms and a running commentary about the boy band references, it's hard to say no. It felt oddly like a sleepover from years ago, except this time there was no chance anyone would wake up with a glitter tattoo stuck to their forehead.

By Friday night, our usual happy hour ritual had been replaced with errands for Teagan's new job. We were buying shoes that met Cinemark's dress code, a bag for her lunch, and waiting while she picked the restaurant. And we didn't mind one bit. There's a comfort in being part of her orbit again, even if it means we're no longer the center of our own.

But as much as we enjoy the noise and the company, we also find ourselves quietly craving the peace we'd grown used to. It's a strange push-and-pull, longing for quiet while savoring the chaos. We'll catch ourselves looking forward to the house being ours again, and then immediately feeling guilty for thinking it.

Empty nest life, it turns out, isn't a straight line. It's a revolving door. Kids come home, leave again, come back for a week, leave for good, come back for a weekend, and leave for good again. Each reentry shifts the dynamic, reshuffles priorities, and reminds us how fluid this stage of life really is.

Maybe that's the new normal. We're learning to live in the in-between—keeping the hum of our empty nest going while embracing the occasional full-house fanfare. And when the quiet returns, because it always does, we'll miss the noise. We'll miss the *Trolls* movie marathons and the Target runs. We'll even miss Miso abandoning us for the floor of Teagan's bedroom because she's clearly the more interesting human.

For now, though, we're leaning into the fullness. The chaos. The laughter spilling from the couch and the shoes kicked off at the door. Because if there's one thing we've learned, it's that the house will be quiet soon enough.

38

Parenting Never Really Ends

Clancy

'd like to say I'm cool, that I've mastered the whole "let them be adults" thing, but then Tanner mentions he hasn't finalized his apartment for law school, and I can feel my blood pressure rising.

It's not that I don't trust him; I do. He's smart, capable, and resourceful. He's 22 years old and about to start a graduate program, for heaven's sake. But there's this part of me, the same part that color-coded chore charts when they were little, that wants to swoop in with grand ideas and to-do lists. Because I know how these things go. If you don't nail down housing early, you're scrambling. And scrambling is the enemy of settled, which is my comfort zone.

Rick is calmer about it, of course. He's confident Tanner will figure it out, while I'm mentally calculating how many days he could live in his old room before we all lose our minds. (Answer: Three, maybe four if he buys dinner.) I know Rick's right—Tanner's got this—but my mom-brain still has its narrative: *What if he waits too long? What if the good apartments are all taken? What if he forgets a security deposit?*

It's the same instinct that bubbles up when Teagan goes to her first day of work at the movie theater in her Cinemark uniform. She's excited, and she's fine. But the part of me that's wired for caretaking wants to follow her there, hand her snacks for break time, and make sure she knows where the mop closet is.

This is the hard part of the empty nest phase, realizing that parenting doesn't end; it just shifts. You still want to offer advice (sometimes unsolicited), still want to cushion the bumps, still want to remind them to wear sunscreen before tubing down a river at 101 degrees. But you also know you have to let go a little more every time.

So I try. I bite my tongue when I want to ask Tanner for the tenth time about his apartment application. I text Teagan a heart emoji instead of "Are you sure you're okay?" I let them stumble a bit when it's safe to stumble, even though it feels unnatural.

Because the truth is, they don't need me to manage their lives anymore. They need me to be a soft place to land when life gets hard. They need me to believe they're capable, even when my nervous system is screaming *fix it, fix it, fix it.*

Parenting never really ends. You just trade the diaper bag for aloe-vera-on-their-sunburn advice and hope they still let you be a part of their lives in ways that matter.

And maybe one day I'll stop hovering in doorways when they're packing up for their next chapter. (Maybe.)

39

Crazel Green and the Passage of Time

Rick

Our street's real name is Hazel Green, but we've been calling it "Crazel Green" for years. It's the kind of nickname that sticks because it's true. We've lived here since 2007, long enough to see every kind of neighborhood drama: ATF raids (yes, really), late-night fireworks, and chaotic pool parties.

But this week, it hit me how much has changed. We went to our neighbor's high school graduation party, and it felt like closing a chapter. She was the last kid from the original pack of "Crazel Green kids," the ones who grew up playing in each other's yards, riding bikes until the streetlights came on, and crowding around our kitchen island like it was the neighborhood cafeteria.

Now they're all grown. Ours included.

It's funny how a place can shift under your feet. Lone Star High School, the one we used to drive past ten times a week for practices and pick-ups, now feels like just another building that slows us down when school's in session. There was a time when it was a landmark of our daily life. Now it's just there.

There's a rhythm to neighborhoods, just like there is to parenting. Kids grow up, graduate, move away, and the life that once revolved around them subtly reorients itself. Sometimes, you barely notice it happening until you're standing at a graduation party, realizing this is the last one.

On the walk home, Clancy and I laughed about how our house used to be a hub of activity and now it's the quietest it's ever been. Miso does his best to fill the void, but he's not much of a conversationalist. We've grown to like the stillness most days. But there are moments, like that night, when I miss the chaos of "Crazel Green."

Maybe that's the thing about this phase of life: You keep losing the familiar and learning to love the new normal. And just when you get comfortable, it changes again.

40

Humor is How We Survive

We watched Jerry Seinfeld's Duke University commencement speech this week. One of his biggest points to the graduates was simple: *Do not lose your sense of humor.* It felt like he was talking directly to us.

Because the truth is, we've been walking through some heavy things lately. Rick's mom passed away, and even though we knew it was coming, the grief has a way of sneaking up and blindsiding you in the middle of an ordinary Tuesday. We're juggling logistics for her memorial, sorting through estate details, and trying to process the emotions of it all, while also showing up for the kids as they launch into their adult lives.

If we didn't have humor, we'd probably collapse under the weight of it.

We've always been the couple who deals with hard things by laughing at inappropriate times. It's our language, our pressure valve. We'll say something sarcastic and immediately follow it with, "I hope no one else heard that," because honestly, it might not land with anyone else. But it works for us.

There's something about being able to make each other laugh, even when it feels like the walls are closing in, that keeps us afloat. When we're knee-deep in conversations about probates and executors and "what on earth is a remainderman again?" we'll crack a joke just to break the tension. And somehow, that moment of levity gives us the strength to keep going.

It's not that we don't take grief seriously. We do. But we've learned that grief and humor can exist in the same breath. In fact, sometimes they need each other.

So we cling to the laughter. We watch Seinfeld speeches. We remember to tease each other when one of us starts spiraling about the kids' schedules or the endless lists of to-dos. We keep reminding ourselves—and the kids, too—that life is messy and beautiful and sometimes deeply unfair. And that if you can still find something to smile about, even in the middle of it, you'll be okay.

Because humor doesn't erase the hard parts, it just makes them survivable.

41

The End of a Long Goodbye

Rick

When you lose a parent after a long illness, you think you're prepared.

You've had years of practice. Years of little goodbyes. Years of watching pieces of them slip away. And then, the moment comes, the actual goodbye, and you realize preparation was a myth.

My mom's Alzheimer's had been stealing her from us in slow motion. There was no single breaking point, just a thousand small fractures. The day she forgot our kids' names. The first time she didn't recognize the house she'd lived in for decades. The last time she called me by my name. By the time she passed, I told myself I was ready. I'd said what I needed to say. I'd sat at her bedside month after month, whispered in her ear, "Whenever you're ready, Mom, we're ready, too."

And I believed it.

But nothing prepared me for the strange quiet that came after the memorial service.

There was a full month between the day she died and the day we buried her. A month packed with Tanner's graduation, Teagan moving back home for the summer, hundreds of photos to sort through, flowers to choose, an obituary to write, and logistical conversations with my sister and mom's husband about everything from food for the reception to the actual run-of-show of the service.

We didn't stop moving. And that was, in some ways, a gift.

Grief is patient—it will wait for you—but busyness can trick you into thinking you're managing it. We had so much to do that we didn't have to sit with the ache.

I remember standing in that church courtyard in Austin, the reception hall finally empty, the cars being loaded, everyone dispersing. It was a muggy June afternoon, the kind of Texas humidity that makes you feel like you're breathing through a wet towel. And I just stood there and thought, *That's it.*

We'd done the thing. The official grieving, the sanctioned rituals, the casseroles and hugs, and "let me know if you need anything." All of it was over.

And that was the moment I felt the loss—not at the memory care facility, not at the graveside, not even in the eulogy I somehow managed to deliver without breaking. It was there, in that quiet parking lot, when the world moved on and I was left standing still.

Clancy and I talked about it on the drive home. She admitted she'd felt it too, that sudden hollowness when the activity stops. "It's like you've been holding your breath for a month," she said, "and now you have to decide if you even want to exhale."

She was right.

Here's the thing: A long goodbye spares you some of the shock, but it doesn't spare you the emptiness. It just delays it.

I'm in my early 50s. Both my parents are gone now. My sister is in her late 40s. Too young, we keep saying, to be at the top of the family tree. At the memorial, I couldn't stop noticing how many of our peers still had their parents. Everyone seemed flanked by moms and dads, and there we were, this little island of orphans in our forties and fifties.

There's a loneliness in that. And it's not just about missing my mom; it's about realizing the generational scaffolding that held us up is gone.

Clancy told me later she noticed the same thing, walking through the reception: "It's like you and your sister are the adults now," she said. "Which is ridiculous because you've been adults for decades. But now you're the *elders*, whether you asked for it or not."

She was right about that, too.

Some days, I don't think about her at all, which feels like a betrayal. Other days, I land in Austin, the city where I grew up and where my mom and dad anchored me for so long, and it crushes me that I'm there without them.

Losing a parent after a long illness doesn't end cleanly. The "long goodbye" makes you think you've done the grieving incrementally, and then you realize you've only been preparing for the moment when you'll finally have to grieve in full.

That's what the walk across the church courtyard taught me: The goodbye is still a goodbye, and I don't have a neat bow to tie on this story. For now, I'm just learning how to live in the part after the after.

42

When Will Rest Come?

We started joking about it around Father's Day, somewhere between the barrage of group texts and the moment Teagan asked if anyone could run out to Jersey Mike's because she was starving after work. (Rick swears he had déjà vu to the kids' high school football games and late-night Whataburger runs.)

We'd been empty nesters for almost a year. We'd learned how to navigate the silence, how to plan dinners for two, how to pick a vacation date without cross-checking anyone else's calendar. And then came summer.

The kids returned home.

We knew this would happen. We wanted this to happen. But we'd just gotten used to a new rhythm— our rhythm—and suddenly we were right back in the familiar swirl of schedules and logistics.

Teagan asking what time we'd be home so she could make plans. The daily texts, "Hey, do we have any headphones lying around?" landing like tiny reminders that our version of rest might be on pause for a while.

The irony, of course, is that we'd just been talking about rest.

Rick had started therapy a few weeks earlier, and one of the first questions his therapist asked was, "What are you doing to rest?"

Cue the awkward silence.

We listed a few small things, but the truth was that even our "rest" usually involved someone else's needs. Travel, for instance, has always been a recharge for us, but lately, every trip had revolved around the kids, extended family, or someone's graduation.

Then the very next morning, the verse of the day popped up: "Let's go off by ourselves to a quiet place and rest a while." (Mark 6:31)

Clancy texted it to Rick. He'd already seen it.

"Okay, God. We get it," she typed.

But the quiet place never materialized.

We kept telling ourselves, *We could rest later. We'll get a window eventually.* But the truth is, we weren't sure how to create rest when life kept pulling us into motion.

Take Tanner's car, for example. He needed one before starting law school. Simple enough, right? Except he was in Arizona, trying to buy a car here, and every call or email to a dealership went unanswered. Weeks passed. We'd ask for updates, and he'd say, "Yeah, I'm on it." Which, technically, he was, just not with the urgency we would've applied.

It wasn't that he couldn't handle it. He could. He just didn't share our timeline or our definition of *done*.

And that's kind of the crux of it. We like things tied up with a bow. We're planners. We like closure. But rest doesn't exactly thrive in an environment where every loose end feels like a personal challenge to be conquered.

The same dynamic played out with Teagan, just in smaller ways. She's the one who still asks, "Is it okay if I go do this?" even though we've told her she doesn't need our permission.

But the "okay" isn't really about permission; it's about consideration. She's learning her boundaries, and we're learning ours.

It's a strange push-and-pull. We love having them home. We really do.

But we're also learning that the empty nest isn't a static thing. It's not like the kids leave and suddenly life opens up with unlimited time and space for rest and spontaneous adventure. We're still parents. We're still part of a family unit. And family, by nature, is messy and overlapping and full of interruptions.

Maybe that's the real shift: redefining what rest even means.

We used to think rest would arrive once the kids were out of the house, once the calendar cleared, once everything was "done." But that's not how life works, and it's definitely not how parenting works.

Rest might not look like a quiet house or a perfectly organized timeline. It might be ten stolen minutes on the porch before dinner. Or laughing with your adult kids about whether you're running a bed and breakfast.

It might even be choosing to let go of control, of the need to tie everything up with a bow, of the illusion that we can keep all the plates spinning forever.

We're not there yet.

But we're learning.

43

The Last-Minute Flight That Changed More Than Our Weekend

We'd already decided we weren't going to Phoenix. Tanner's birthday was on a Wednesday. He had plans with friends, and we'd "celebrate later." We put it on the shelf, which is Clancy's shorthand for *move on, don't dwell.*

And we really did try to move on. We sent him a cookie cake (shout out to Insomnia Cookies—sponsor us already), covered the dinner tab for his friends, and told ourselves this was normal. Our parents didn't come to every birthday. Kids grow up. It's fine.

Except it wasn't fine. Not really.

Clancy: I'm big on birthdays. I started celebrating them "big" when the kids were little, and it just stuck. Missing one, even at 22, felt like I was letting him down somehow. I tried to be chill. I'm not great at chill.

Rick could sense it. He has a radar for this kind of thing after 24 years of marriage—the subtle signs I'm struggling, even when I'm pretending I'm not. By Thursday morning, he texted me:

"How impulsive do you feel like being? Might be time to flex that muscle…"

Rick: I was half-joking. Mostly. But I'd already started looking at flights. Once you dive into Amex points and airline alliances, you either go all in or you give up. I was not going to give up.

By 2:00 p.m., we had two first-class tickets to Phoenix, cheaper in points than economy, thanks to some travel gymnastics Rick will happily nerd out about if you let him. Twenty-four hours later, we were hugging Tanner outside his apartment.

The impulsiveness we used to fantasize about is suddenly available. And yet, we don't always use it.

We'll bend over backward to show up for the kids. But for ourselves, we'll wait. We'll plan. We'll say "someday."

Rick: That hit me mid-flight. Why do we jump at a chance to rearrange life for Tanner but not for the two of us?

The Phoenix trip was everything we hoped it would be: simple, quick, and joyfully unplanned. We hit the Lobby Bar at the Ambassador Hotel (great people-watching, if you like spotting bachelorette parties in lingerie-as-tops), had dinner at Buck & Rider, where they surprised Tanner with his name flashing on the old-school flipboard sign, and walked through Papago Park the next morning before flying home.

It wasn't about the food or the scenery, though. It was about the reminder: We can still do this. We can choose adventure for ourselves, not just for the kids.

Clancy: I did it for Tanner but also for me. I needed that hug, that moment to see him thriving. But it also filled my heart. Maybe that's what we forget sometimes: The things we think are for them often matter just as much for us.

We came home lighter, not just because of the desert sun but because we'd flexed a muscle we'd let atrophy. That impulsive, "why not?" part of us that used to say yes to road trips and cheap flights and dinners that ran too late on a school night.

We want more of that.

So, consider this our public reminder: Next time we feel the pull to wait, to delay, to shelf the idea, we're going to remember Phoenix. And maybe book the flight anyway.

44

Exxiety and Other New Emotions

We were sitting in the same movie theater where, years ago, we'd watched the first *Inside Out* with Teagan. Back then, she was still little enough that standing in line for tickets felt like a family adventure. She remembered eating dinner in the theater lobby that night because we couldn't risk losing our seats. (This was before reserved seating, which now feels as antiquated as dial-up internet.)

Fast-forward to *Inside Out 2*. Same theater. But now we're empty nesters; our daughter is the one scanning our discounted tickets because she works at the concession stand. The full-circle moment wasn't lost on us.

As the credits rolled, we found ourselves asking: What would *Inside Out: Empty Nest Edition* look like? Which emotions have been at the controls since the kids left home?

Rick

Some emotions would definitely get promoted. Nostalgia, for one. She's already waiting in the wings in *Inside Out 2*, a little old lady with a shawl, itching to run the board. Empty nest life is basically her big break. Suddenly, you can't walk through the kitchen without tripping over some memory of "when the kids were small," usually triggered by a random object like a half-broken lunchbox you can't bring yourself to throw away.

Then there's what Clancy calls "external anxiety," or, as I dubbed it, "exxiety." (It's harder to pronounce than it looks, but I stand by it.) This is the kind of anxiety pointed outward at your kids when they're not under your roof. Will they drive home safely? Will the boat flip over? Will they make wise choices at that party? It's like the normal anxiety we used to have, only now we can't physically see them, which makes it 37 times worse.

Clancy

And some emotions fade into the background. Embarrassment? Don't even know her. At this stage, I'm not losing sleep over what people think. I'll happily wear my glasses and sweatpants to the grocery store because who cares? The same goes for FOMO. There was a time when missing a dinner or event would have gutted me. Now, I'll happily stay home and scroll through pictures of the thing I missed.

But then there are the sneaky ones. Cynicism, for example. It shows up at the edges when the news feels bleak, when people drive like maniacs, or when we start to feel invisible at dinner parties. It can take over the controls if we're not careful.

Which is why we've decided optimism needs a bigger voice on the control panel. Not the toxic "just think happy thoughts!" version but the kind where we actively notice the good around us. The neighbor's blooming tree. The trail near our house. The fact that our kids still call us, even when they don't need money.

Honestly, it sounds like a decent cast.

45

First Apartment Arguments

We thought we'd graduated from staging areas. You know, the stacks of bins and boxes over-taking your living room, each labeled in Sharpie like a pop-up distribution center. Turns out, we hadn't.

This summer, the guest room looked like a small branch of Bed Bath & Beyond had exploded. Teagan's moving into her first college apartment, Tanner into his first unfurnished "adult" apartment, and every corner of our house was stacked with "essentials." Sheets for her queen. Measuring cups for his kitchen. IKEA boxes lined up like soldiers waiting for deployment.

This situation is basically a master class in negotiating who you are as parents—and as a couple.

Rick (big-picture thinker, low on decorative pillows): "He's 22. Shouldn't he be the one picking out the throw pillows?" Clancy (detail-oriented, loves a good tablescape): "He's 22 and in summer classes two states away. He literally asked me to handle it. And by the way, he's lived with me for 22 years. He trusts me."

This was the rhythm all summer. Rick wanted Tanner to make his own decisions, to feel the weight of independence. Clancy, well, she just wanted his kitchen to have actual utensils and maybe a vacuum cleaner that didn't require duct tape.

It's funny how first apartments pull you right back into old arguments with a new twist. Rick remembers his first apartment vividly: one nice couch, a lot of mix-and-match furniture, and nights sitting on the floor because there was no TV stand. Independence forged through lack.

"Do the chairs even need to match?" Rick would ask. "Yes," Clancy would answer, "because life is nicer when chairs match."

These were "healthy discussions," as we kept calling them, and they'd pop up everywhere, from the IKEA showroom to our text threads with Tanner, who would respond to our barrage of photos with a casual, "Sure. Whatever works."

And maybe that's the hardest part: The kids aren't here to hash this out with you. Tanner's not strolling the aisles at HomeGoods, debating bathmat colors. He's outsourcing his taste, or lack thereof, to us. That left us debating not just which coffee table to buy but how much we were shaping his adult life versus simply supporting it.

There's no tidy answer. Parenting adult kids is like trying to stand on a moving escalator; you're always recalibrating.

But we did figure out a few things along the way, like the fact that we're both done with DIY moving marathons. Thirty years ago, we would have loaded every box and driven a U-Haul ourselves. This time, we booked movers before we even bought the first set of measuring cups.

We also realized these "first apartment arguments" weren't really about furniture at all. They were about watching our son step into a new life while still wanting to protect and care for him. It's a delicate dance.

So, yes, Tanner's new couch matches the coffee table. And yes, Rick had to let go of his "mismatched is fine" philosophy for the sake of marital harmony. But the truth is, we're both just hoping that when he walks into that apartment for the first time, he feels at home.

Because that's really what this is all about. Not the chairs. Not the pillows. But creating a soft landing as they launch.

(For the record, he still doesn't care about the pillows.)

46

A Little More Kindness Wouldn't Hurt

We weren't planning to spiral into a big-picture reflection on humanity. We were just catching up over coffee, scrolling through the news like you do—one headline about an assassination attempt, another about Richard Simmons and Dr. Ruth passing away—and somewhere between the grief and the absurdity, one of us said, "When did kindness become such a rare commodity?"

(For the record, Rick actually said "civil discourse," which is very on brand for him. Clancy immediately countered with "kindness," which is equally on brand.)

It sounds dramatic, we know. The world has always been messy. But lately, it feels like we're all sharper around the edges. The driver who cuts you off without a courtesy wave. The movie theater rows left looking like a landfill because, hey, someone else will clean it up. Even the way we scroll online—so quick to dismiss someone's whole existence over one opinion.

We keep joking that outrage has become a business model. And business is booming.

But there's a cost to living in this constant simmer of frustration. We feel it in ourselves, too. It's easier to retreat into our little bubble, to convince ourselves we're "too busy" to care about anyone else's experience. We've definitely been guilty of that, especially when life was jam-packed with kid schedules and we were just trying to survive the day.

Now, though, life is quieter. We have the time and space to notice things we used to brush past, like how one small kindness can change the tone of an entire day. When someone holds the door open, it actually stops us for a second. We'll look at each other and go, *See? It's not that hard.*

We're trying to be those people more often, the ones who slow down. We've started small: actually making eye contact with the person at the checkout counter, letting someone merge in traffic even when they waited until the very last second (and Rick's blood pressure rises in protest), and asking the waiter how their day is going and actually listening to the answer.

Does it fix the world? Of course not. But it softens the edges.

And maybe that's what this stage of life is asking of us. When the house empties out, you can either double down on disconnection or you can decide to be the thing you wish you saw more of. We'd love to say it's easy, but sometimes, it takes a conscious pause, especially when we're already halfway through a rant about how "people have lost all sense of common decency."

A little more kindness wouldn't hurt. And if we're lucky, maybe it's contagious.

47

Manifesting Optimism

We've started calling this the *Bummer Summer*.

It's not that everything was awful—there were bright spots—but wow, it felt like life was taking attendance and calling out everyone we love for a round of challenges. Illness swept through our house (pink eye, of all things, which neither of us had seen since the days of sharing juice boxes at elementary school). Rick's mom passed away. Friends endured the unimaginable loss of a child. Our neighbors were hit with something you wouldn't wish on anyone. Even the daily news seemed intent on sucking any remaining joy from the room.

We found ourselves teetering on the edge of cynicism, that little voice that whispers, "Why bother expecting good things?"

And yet, there's this image we keep coming back to.

It's an image we stumbled on while talking about optimism one afternoon. Picture it: a giant, awkward elephant launching itself into the air, ears flapping, eyes wide, and on the other side of the trapeze bar is a monkey—half its size, maybe a tenth its weight—reaching out its tiny hands. By all logic, this should end badly.

And yet.

The elephant believes. The monkey believes. And somehow, that belief makes the impossible possible.

It sounds ridiculous, because it is, but it's the perfect picture of what it feels like to hope for something you can't control. Life as an empty nester can feel a little like that trapeze act: You're leaping into a phase you've never been in before, and you can't be entirely sure what's waiting on the other side.

Rick: Optimism is the antidote to cynicism. It's what keeps us from focusing on the tree in the middle of the road and slamming into it.

Clancy: Okay, but you know me. I'm not exactly Mrs. Manifestation. It's hard not to zero in on the tree when it's right there.

We get it. We've lived it. This summer, when we were helping Tanner move into his new apartment, we led with exhaustion instead of gratitude.

Moving an adult child across states isn't for the faint of heart. There's the logistical chaos: Did we remember the clicker for the parking garage? No. Did we get locked out and have to track down a security guard? Yes. There's the physical toll: IKEA trips, curtain rods, narrow staircases, repeat. And then there's the emotional push and pull of watching your child step into a brand-new life while you're, quite literally, left holding the packing tape.

There were moments where we wanted to collapse in a heap of "this is too much." But then Tanner texted us at 4:17 a.m.

> "I just paged through the picture book Teagan made me before I started at ASU, and I'm genuinely sobbing. I love this family so, so, so much. It hurts to leave my faux family in Arizona, but I can't wait to see y'all."

And there it was: the thing we could choose to focus on.

Because optimism isn't about pretending everything's fine when it isn't, it's about focusing on the love we've instilled in our kids instead of the 12 trips back to At Home. It's about letting the gratitude moments take up more space than the frustrating ones.

Clancy: Which is harder than it sounds. Cynicism sneaks in like a stray cat. You don't even remember letting it inside.

Rick: Exactly. That's why you have to feed optimism on purpose.

We realized we needed to start manifesting optimism, not in the "cheeseburger will appear if I visualize it hard enough" way, but in the grounded, practical sense.

We've started taking news fasts when the negativity overload gets too heavy. Rick used to be the guy who had the *New York Times* thrown at his dorm room door in college; he's always loved staying up to date on the news. But lately, scrolling headlines feels like letting someone dump a bag of wet sand on our shoulders every morning. So we take breaks. We turn off the TV, stay off the apps, and let ourselves remember that the world is still full of good things even if they aren't breaking news.

We're also learning to lead with gratitude when we tell the story of a hard day. Like when we came home from setting up Tanner's apartment, it would have been easy to open with, "We're so tired, our backs hurt, and we nearly strangled each other over where to hang the curtains." But instead, we're practicing starting with the wins: "We got him settled. He's ready for law school. We did it."

And we've started asking each other this simple question: *What are we choosing to remember?*

Are we going to rehash the flight delay or talk about the amazing trip? Are we going to dwell on the sore backs or the fact that we got to create a soft landing for Tanner as he steps into his next chapter? Are we going to fixate on the frustrating security guard who made us jump through hoops to get into his building, or are we going to focus on the gratitude that he wanted us there and that we have the kind of family connection where he actually *invites* us into his space?

It's a mindset shift. And some days, we're better at it than others. But it's the kind of practice that, little by little, starts to change the way you see everything else.

It's a choice, every time.

At this point, we've lived enough life to know that the world will always offer us reasons to despair. But we've also lived enough to know that optimism—real, deliberate optimism—is what allows us to keep building something new.

This fall, we're dreaming about what's next for us: expanding our podcast, writing this book, maybe even going into business together. (Rick is optimistic. Clancy is… cautiously optimistic.) Most businesses fail, and adding the marriage component could be combustible, but we keep coming back to the trapeze elephant.

One of us leaps. The other catches.

We can't promise we'll stick the landing every time, but we're choosing to believe we'll find our way across.

And as for which of us is the elephant and which is the monkey?

Rick knows better than to touch that one.

48

Wisdom From Our Elders

Clancy

Bunny looked at us across the table, her hands folded neatly, her expression as neutral as if we'd asked her to pass the salt.

"It was different having him home all the time," she said.

Rick snorted out a laugh before he could stop himself. I followed because there was no hiding the brilliance of her delivery. Phil, to his credit, just grinned and shook his head. Fifty-seven years of marriage had taught him that some lines need no follow-up.

"That's going in the book," Rick said, and Phil raised his coffee mug like he was fine with that.

We were sitting in our dining room with my parents, Phil and Bunny, BiBi and Pop Pop to our kids, recording an episode of *The Loud Quiet*. The mics were set up, but honestly, it felt more like sneaking into a secret chamber of wisdom than a podcast. Phil and Bunny have been through this season already, the one we're just now navigating. They'd launched all three kids, adjusted to an empty house, retired, stayed married, and managed to do it with a grace that seemed effortless. We'd invited them over to tell us how.

It turned out, they didn't really understand the premise.

"We never called ourselves empty nesters," Bunny said when we asked about it. She shrugged, like she was brushing lint off her sweater. "We just had more freedom. More time to do things we wanted to do."

I shot Rick a look. We've spent the past year dissecting the phrase "empty nest," talking about how hard it is, how quiet it can be, and how lonely it can feel. And here were my parents, sitting across the table, utterly unmoved by the whole concept.

Phil leaned forward, elbows on the table. "We didn't think of it as a category," he said. "We just kept living."

I wanted to argue. I wanted to tell them it isn't that simple. But the truth is, they didn't seem to be oversimplifying. They'd simply never stopped.

They talked about their friends—the ones they've had for decades, the ones who didn't disappear when the soccer games and choir concerts ended. "We've been at the same church for 32 years," Bunny said. "Those friendships stick. You grow up together. You take care of each other."

Rick gave a low whistle. "Thirty-two years. We've moved three times in the past ten."

"Loneliness will eat you alive," Phil said. He didn't say it like a warning, just a fact. "You need people around you. People who know you."

I thought about the parents we'd shared bleachers with, the ones who'd dropped out of our lives as soon as the kids graduated. There's no malice in it; it's just what happens when the glue holding you together dissolves. But Phil and Bunny had built something deeper, and it showed.

We circled back to Bunny's opening line because we needed more. What does "different" actually mean when your spouse retires and is suddenly home all the time?

Phil laughed before he answered. "I was used to having deadlines," he said. "And I'd ask Bunny to do things for me, the way I did at work. She'd look at me and say, 'Can't you do that yourself?'"

Bunny smirked. "He was messing up my schedule."

We laughed, but I felt a pang of recognition. It's easy to imagine how the quiet of the empty nest could be disrupted by one person trying to find their footing while the other has already found theirs.

"It takes time," Phil said. "We worked it out. You just work it out."

He said it like that, no five-step plan, no big revelation. And maybe that's the point. They didn't host a family retreat to plan their empty nest strategy. They just kept living.

And living, for them, looks like movement. Travel they'd never had time for when the kids were home: Israel, Germany, New Zealand. Vacations with the grandkids, who each get to pick a destination when they turn ten. Pickleball at the neighborhood tennis court. Phil belongs to a chainsaw crew for disaster relief. Bunny volunteers at the church's donation center, sorting clothes and helping women find what they need with the same care she once packed school lunches. They mentor. They show up. They say yes.

"We had a bucket list," Bunny said. "And we finally had time for it."

Before they left, we asked for the one piece of advice they'd give couples like us, stepping into this season. Bunny didn't hesitate. "Do things together. Keep enjoying each other's company. Stay active."

Phil added, "Don't stop. Don't stop trying. Be creative. Try new things, even if it's ziplining in Costa Rica. We never thought we'd do that. But we did."

We stood in the doorway and watched them walk to their car, hand in hand like they have been since before we were born. Fifty-seven years. It's easy to look at that and imagine some grand secret holding it all together. But maybe the secret is smaller than we think.

Maybe you just keep showing up. You keep try-ing. You keep saying yes.

And when life shifts, as it always will, you work it out.

49

The Empty Nest Olympics

We didn't get invited to the actual Olympics (a tragic oversight, clearly). No parades, no torch, no shiny uniforms with complicated zippers. Instead, we decided to host our own: *the Empty Nest Olympics*. Our version has no track, no parallel bars, and no closing ceremonies. But we *do* have events.

This started as a joke. One night, we were talking about how we were doing at this whole "life after kids" thing and realized we were basically grading ourselves. Were we making friends? Planning date nights? Or were we just sitting around scrolling on our phones? We had wins and losses, so naturally, we turned it into a game.

Instead of pole vaults and synchronized diving, our events are things like *making new friends* (harder than the high jump), *planning trips* (which require Olympic-level follow-through), and *not losing our minds in a house that suddenly feels too quiet*. There are medals involved, but we hand them out ourselves, and truth be told, they're mostly metaphorical.

Event 1: Maintaining and Making Friends

This one's two events in one: keeping the friendships you already have and building new ones.

Clancy: Maintaining friendships? Gold medal, no question. I'm good at staying connected with people I love. We're the house that texts neighbors on a random Friday night: "Hey, y'all home? Come over." That's how we ended up watching the Olympic opening ceremonies with friends the other night. Smooth sailing.

Rick: I'll give myself silver. I'm comfortable being alone, and it's easy to think, *Oh, I'll text the guys later*, but then later turns into never. I even delegate it to Clancy sometimes: "Hey, have you reached out to them?" It's not great.

Making new friends? That's trickier. Without kids creating automatic social circles, it's like we've forgotten how to do it. The built-in connection points are gone: the ballgames, the PTA, the graduation parties. And we're left realizing that as adults, it's not like you can just walk up to someone at the grocery store and ask, "Do you want to be my friend?"

We've tried. We started an empty nest life group at church and met some great new people, but it's slow-going. Clancy compared it to walking into the Olympic village and realizing you've been training for the wrong sport. You know you're there for something, but it's not exactly clear what, and everyone else seems to already have a team.

Rick: Honestly, I have to push myself. Left to my own devices, I'd be perfectly content sitting alone on the porch with a bourbon. But then I read another study last week that said friendships in your later years are one of the biggest factors in longevity—bigger than smoking, bigger than diet. So apparently, I have to make small talk to live longer. Great.

Event 2: Planning Dates and Trips

In the early days of the empty nest, we filled our weekends on purpose: dinner reservations, weekend trips, even spontaneous getaways. If the calendar looked empty, we fixed it.

Clancy: It was the right move. We suddenly found ourselves staring at wide-open time, and instead of sitting around the house wondering what the kids were doing, we got out. We started strong. Really strong.

Rick: But lately, I'd have to give myself, maybe bronze. I'm good at thinking about trips: Big Sky, Tahiti, the Caymans. I've researched them all, but the follow-through isn't always there. Dinner out is my fallback plan, and sometimes even that feels like a stretch.

The truth is, it's easy to slip into a rut. Everything became "Arizona or Austin," which isn't bad (both places are lovely), but it wasn't exactly creative. We kept saying, "After the kids are settled, we'll plan more." But at some point, you realize that's just an excuse.

Planning dates and trips isn't about being Instagram-perfect. It's about staying intentional. And for us, that's work because the easy default is to stay home, order takeout, and scroll, which is fine sometimes. But we both know that when we get lazy about connection, it shows up everywhere else, too.

Event 3: Discovering New Hobbies

This event was almost a total disaster.

Clancy: We didn't even qualify for the team. The pickleball set is still in the closet, mocking us. We talked about hobbies, but we didn't do anything with it.

Then we remembered the podcast.

Clancy: Oh, right. The podcast started as a hobby. We were trying to find something that connected us, and we went all in. That's a gold medal right there.

Rick: Exactly. We didn't need ten new hobbies. We needed one thing we could do together that we actually enjoyed. And the podcast checks that box. Plus, it forces us to have real conversations every week, which is bonus points.

Event 4: Communicating With Each Other

This was the one event where we stood on the podium together.

Rick: I said silver at first because I hate saying "perfect." But Clancy convinced me: gold. We talk. We've always carved out time for each other, even when the kids were little. We put them to bed early. We asked our parents to babysit so we could go on dates. Those habits made this transition a lot smoother.

Clancy: I've watched couples struggle because once the kids leave, they have nothing to say to each other. That hasn't been our story. We can just sit and talk about anything, not just the kids. And the podcast forces us into those deeper conversations, which is a bonus.

That doesn't mean we're world record holders. There's room to grow, especially on conflict-heavy topics. But the fact that we can give ourselves gold here is huge because it's the one event that makes all the others easier.

Event 5: Dreaming About the Future

This is our strongest category. World record level.

Rick: Thinking about the future is fun for me. When life feels like drudgery, dreaming big pulls me out of it. Sure, most of my future-planning revolves around travel—Nepal, overwater bungalows, you name it—but it's not really about the trips. It's about creating a vision for what's next.

Clancy: And I love that about us. We've been asking each other, "Where do you see us in five years?" since our anniversary dinners in our twenties. Some of those dreams happened. Some didn't. But the dreaming itself has shaped who we are and where we've ended up.

We even joke about it with our kids. One of them has inherited the "I'm going to do this" mindset (not "want to," not "maybe," just "I'm going to"). And we love it because dreaming big is contagious.

We talk a lot about how dreams overshoot what's possible. But that's the point. When you dream big, even if you don't hit the exact target, you land in a pretty incredible place.

The funny thing about grading ourselves was realizing the medals didn't really matter. The point was the conversation.

It reminded us of the areas that need attention, like making new friends and planning intentional time together, and it reminded us of the strengths that carry us through.

Without dreaming together, we'd probably feel like we were just treading water. Without communicating, we'd drift apart. Without at least trying to make friends, we'd end up in our little bubble.

And the good news? The Empty Nest Olympics aren't a one-time event. We get to keep competing. We get to keep getting better.

50

Losing (and Reclaiming) the Empty Nest

We didn't even notice it happening at first. One day, we were blissfully leaning into the freedom of empty-nest life, taking impromptu date nights, making spontaneous plans, and remembering what it felt like to be responsible only for ourselves.

And then, somewhere between summer colds, Fourth of July fireworks, and planning dinners around Teagan's work schedule, we realized that we'd slipped right back into kid-focused mode.

Our house looked like a supply depot. Conversations that used to drift toward travel plans or dinner ideas now revolved around car shopping, lease agreements, and where to find twin XL sheets. Every room had a staging area. We'd lost the empty nest and hadn't even seen it go.

"I feel like we're just living the kids' lives right now," one of us finally said.

"Yeah," the other replied. "We need to figure out how to get back to being empty nesters; otherwise, we don't even have a podcast anymore."

It was funny in that not-really-funny way.

The truth is, it's easy to let the kids creep back into the center. There's always something—school, jobs, apartments, vacations—that feels urgent, that needs your attention. Add in the gravitational pull of old habits, and suddenly you're knee-deep in their lives again.

We saw it clearly on the Fourth of July. Both of us were recovering from being sick. It was blazing hot. Neither kid was around. We sat at home debating whether to make the effort to see fireworks.

Eight-fifty rolled around, and we finally rallied, drove up to a nearby bridge, and watched a drone show.

"You were excited at first," Clancy reminded Rick.

"Until I realized I was watching a glorified screensaver," Rick deadpanned. "Give me real fireworks any day."

It struck us later: Maybe that drone show was a metaphor. There's the glossy, pre-programmed version of life, and then there's the real thing—the messy, unpredictable fireworks. We wanted more fireworks.

So, the next night, we took ourselves on a date, if you can call Chili's a date.

We sat at a high-top in the bar, ordered burgers and margaritas, and texted Teagan a picture just to rile her up. (It worked. "You went to Chili's without me?!")

It wasn't glamorous. The fries were great, the burgers were overcooked, and the whole thing felt a little nostalgic, like the youth group dinners we'd go to in our teens. But it was exactly what we needed: a reset. A reminder that we could still choose each other, even when life felt overrun by everyone else's schedules and needs.

The kids will keep pulling us in, and that's okay. They're still ours, after all. But the more we practice, the better we get at stepping back out and finding our rhythm again.

That's the thing about empty nesting; it's not a static state you achieve and then coast. You have to keep reclaiming it, again and again, in big ways and small ones.

Sometimes, that looks like planning a weekend getaway. Other times, it's just choosing a random Tuesday night at Salsa (our neighborhood Mexican place), laughing over chips and salsa, and remembering why you actually like each other.

Because we like the fireworks, and we don't want to miss them.

51

We Still Like Each Other

We sat down the night before our 24th anniversary with a laptop, a bottle of wine, and a box of old photos. Honestly, it felt a little like marriage archaeology.

The first photo that stopped us was from the engagement trip to Costa Rica, back when Rick still had a full head of hair and Clancy still thought she was in control of her schedule. Rick had somehow pulled off the surprise of a lifetime. He'd sent Clancy a packet of instructions ahead of time: what to pack, when to be at the airport, and what to expect. At the time, she was working as a flight attendant in Baltimore and living in a "crash pad," airline slang for an overcrowded group apartment where ten crew members rotated through bunks between flights. The morning she was supposed to leave, her alarm didn't go off, and she ended up sprinting down a massive hill with her luggage, convinced she was going to miss the flight. She made it, barely, and when they met in Miami, Rick led her onto a plane bound for Costa Rica. A few days later, in a flower-filled room, he knelt down and asked her to marry him.

Then came the wedding day. At the time, we were convinced that getting married on Memorial Day weekend would guarantee romantic three-day getaways forever.

(Ha. That's cute. Ask us about all the anniversaries we've spent sweating on the sidelines of Memorial Day soccer tournaments with off-brand Yeti cups in our hands.)

Looking at those pictures, we laughed at how blissfully unaware Clancy had been in the bridal suite while Rick and the groomsmen huddled in the church offices with a weather radio blaring updates about a storm system bearing down. "If it rains on your wedding day, it's good luck," people say. We figured a tornado must mean we were really set for life.

There was a whole string of pictures from our early anniversaries. Our first anniversary in Hawaii, when we were tanned and childless and convinced that big, exotic trips would be the norm every year. (Spoiler: They weren't.) There were the baby years, when an "anniversary celebration" meant wrangling a babysitter, scarfing down dinner at a restaurant, and collapsing on the couch as soon as we got home. We laughed at the hairstyles and the pleated pants, but the exhaustion was written all over our faces in those photos.

And then there was *that* picture from Seasons 52. The one where we're smiling for the camera through gritted teeth because we'd just had one of those dumb, escalating fights you can't even remember the root of later. We'd been seated in a back corner of the restaurant, Rick got snippy about it, Clancy snapped back, and the rest of the night spiraled. We made it through the meal, but we didn't talk to each other the entire car ride home.

Rick: I remember thinking, *Is this what we've become, just co-managers of a household who can't make it through a dinner without biting each other's heads off?*

Clancy: I thought the same thing. I hated the distance I felt, but I didn't know how to bridge it in that moment.

The photos from Napa and Thailand told a different story. Those trips weren't just vacations; they were lifelines. In Napa, we rented a convertible, toured wineries, and pretended for a weekend that the stress we were carrying at home didn't exist. We took the cheesy group limo tour, sipping wine with strangers we'll never see again, but it gave us space to breathe and remember who we were outside of being parents.

Thailand was even bigger. We stayed with Clancy's brother in Bangkok for a few days before heading out to the beaches of Koh Samui. On paper, it was a dream trip: white sand, turquoise water, street food that cost less than a latte at home. But underneath the beauty, we knew we needed that time as a couple. We weren't just sightseeing; we were recalibrating, trying to find our rhythm again.

Looking through all those pictures—the big trips, the soccer-field anniversaries, the baby years, the dumb fights—we saw the full arc of "us." And here's what surprised us most: We like who we are now.

Rick: I actually like this version of us better than the twenty-something version. We're lighter. We laugh more. We don't get stuck in the little stuff the way we used to.

Clancy: We still fight. We still annoy each other in Nebraska Furniture Mart. But we don't stay there. We can say, "Hey, that was snippy," and move on. That's new for us. Ten years ago, we might have stayed mad for days.

It didn't just happen. When the kids left, we made a decision to "exercise our relationship muscles" again. We forced ourselves to book dinner reservations, even when it felt easier to stay home. We went on weekend trips to Fort Worth, not because we're obsessed with Fort Worth, but because we needed to relearn how to be just the two of us again. We had to rebuild the friendship that got buried under two decades of parenting.

And now, after living this empty-nest rhythm for a while, we can finally say it out loud: *We still like each other.*

Not in a smug way. More in a grateful, holy-cow-we-made-it-through-the-hard-stuff way. Because there were seasons, especially those long, exhausting years of little kids and constant stress, when we weren't sure we'd make it here. We know plenty of couples who didn't.

But here's what we've learned: You can't coast into this. You can't assume that just because you've been together 20 years, you'll magically enjoy the quiet when the house empties. You have to be intentional. You have to build a marriage that can hold its own without the gravitational pull of parenting.

Clancy: That word—intentional—gets thrown around a lot, but it's true. We choose to invest in "us," even when it's awkward, even when it's easier to scroll on our phones in separate rooms.

Rick: I like us. I like that we can spend an entire Saturday running errands—mattress shopping, looking at apartments for Tanner—and not kill each other. I like that we can sit in these chairs and banter back and forth without needing the kids around to fill the silence. Ten years ago, I'm not sure we could have done that.

This isn't the kind of thing you slap on a motivational poster (though Rick did accidentally craft a calendar-worthy line): *The memories of the past help reignite the excitement of the present and secure the stability of the future.*

Clancy: I'm putting that on a T-shirt, maybe with a cat hanging from a tree.

But it's true. Looking back at where we've been makes us appreciate where we are.

We're not perfect. We'll still fight about dumb things. We'll still annoy each other. But we like each other. And that's the foundation we're carrying into this next chapter.

Rick: I like us now. More than I ever have. And I want to keep liking us for the next 24 years.

Clancy: Same.

Acknowledgments

We never thought a book would be a part of our journey in the empty nest, but here we are. When we started our podcast in 2023, we saw it as a way to stay connected as a couple. We stepped out of our comfort zone to attend Podfest in January 2025, and that's where we discovered we had something bigger than what we had started in our former playroom upstairs at home.

We'd like to thank Tina Dietz of Twin Flames Studios (whom we met in line at the Podpage booth) for hearing what our podcast was about and immediately telling us it needed to be a book. She gave us the confidence and vision to see that a book could be a reality.

Thank you to Michelle Fishering of Alembic Press for taking our ideas and episodes and transforming them into the essays they have become. You really understood what we wanted to share with our audience of Empty Nesters.

Our podcast has been greatly improved thanks to the help of Marc Ronick of iRonick Media. His coaching made us realize we can turn this hobby into something more.

Thank you to our listeners of *The Loud Quiet - Empty Nest Living* podcast. Some of you have been with us from the beginning, and we appreciate your dedication. Our reach has grown, and we thank you for suggesting us to your friends, family, co-workers, and random people you meet who are going through this phase of life.

Some of these stories would not have been possible without our early guests, all of whom are friends of ours. Thank you, Ward and Ashley DuLaney, JP and Aeryn Shiffer, and Jim and Ibby Gill. Thank you for trusting us to share your stories and for being our guinea pigs.

We need to put in a special shout-out to Ashley DuLaney, who has been there for what feels like the beginning of time. She's seen us at our best and worst and was totally invested in our new path.

Our first photo shoot was done by our friend and neighbor, Shayla Ally. She heard our vision and put together some great shots that we used for our first logo. She has been a constant supporter of us, and we thank her for that.

Brandy, Bryan, Scott, and Eileen, friends in our Empty Nesters Life Group, have kept us going and provided anecdotes along the way. We appreciate you!

Good neighbors make for a good life. Thanks, Eric and Jim, for being excellent neighbors, willing to raise a glass while sitting on the porch, lend a hand when something goes awry, and always being ready with a shovel, no questions asked. And thanks to Ibby for always bringing the awesome hummus dip to our impromptu happy hours, which often extend into late nights.

The Real Cheer Moms—Laura, Aubre, Amber, Sarah, and Kim—thank you for being a sounding board and constant source of support in life for so many years.

Miso, our daughter's cat that lives in our house. You can be super frustrating, but you have supplied ample hours of entertainment (even a few appearances on the podcast) and fodder for stories. We will miss you when you go live with Teagan.

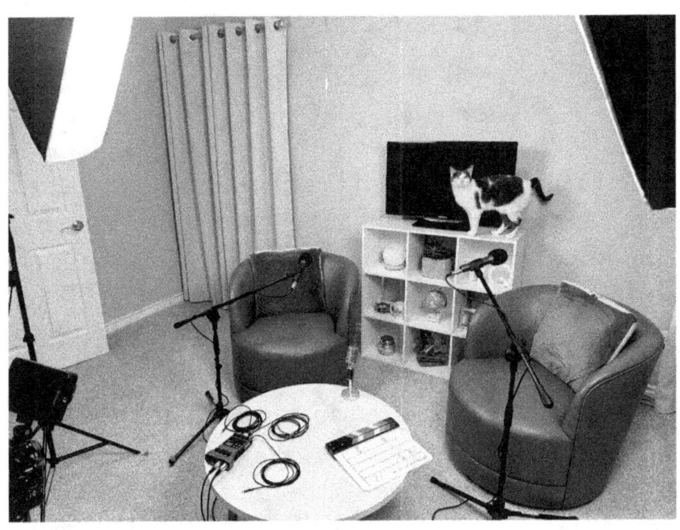

We have great examples of what empty nest living should look like. Thank you to our parents, Bunny and Phil Esch and Linda and Richard Denton. Rick's parents are no longer with us, but they showed us how to enjoy life after the kids left the nest. Clancy's parents remain a constant "relationship goals" couple and continue to be our biggest cheerleaders in all our endeavors. They have also taught us how to be great at being grandparents (when our time comes).

Tanner and Teagan, our kiddos, have been so excited about this project since it was just a thought. Thank you for letting us share stories, the good and the bad, about your lives. You guys make us so proud. We are so lucky to have been blessed with such great human beings, whom we get to watch navigate life. Thank you for being so encouraging when we decided to pivot into the world of podcasting and for still wanting to spend time with us.

Clancy: When I approached Rick with the idea of starting a podcast about empty-nest life, I wasn't sure what the response would be. He was fully on board, and I am so proud of what we have built together. I could not have asked for a better partner in business and life. You are an amazing father, and our kiddos are so lucky to have you as their dad. Through all the ups and downs that come with life, we have managed to keep each other laughing. There have been tears, some even shed on the podcast, but my life is so much better because you are in it. Let's keep this going for many more years; there are still so many places we haven't seen yet.

Rick: Clancy, you are the original muse for *The Loud Quiet*. There is no idea, there is no podcast, there is no book, there isn't even the name *The Loud Quiet* without you. Your willingness to be vulnerable and force the risky and raw conversations provided the space for this idea to emerge. Even when we spar creatively, I come out of it knowing that what we generated is better than what I could have done alone. I love working with you and how that has brought us even closer together. I'm a better man, parent, human, and hopefully husband because of you. These empty nest years have been fantastic so far, and I'm so excited to see how we'll continue to thrive in this empty nest life going forward. I can't think of anyone I'd want to partner with on this creative and business endeavor more than you.

Stay Connected

Learn more about *The Loud Quiet* and sign up for the newsletter by visiting

www.theloudquiet.com

Searchable episode list for *The Loud Quiet* podcast:

www.theloudquiet.com/episodes/

Join the conversation in *The Loud Quiet* community:

www.theloudquiet.com/community

About the Authors

Rick and Clancy Denton are empty nesters embracing what's next with a blend of nostalgia, curiosity, humor, and a shared sense of adventure. With their two young adult kids out of the house, they've reconnected as a couple and are leaning fully into this vibrant season of life.

On their podcast, *The Loud Quiet - Empty Nest Living,* they explore what it means to thrive in the empty nest years, navigating changing routines, launching new ventures, rediscovering each other, and laughing through the unexpected moments that come with this new stage. It's real; from snort laughs to sobbing, it's just two people figuring things out together

www.ingramcontent.com/pod-product-compliance
Lightning Source LLC
Chambersburg PA
CBHW071211240726
48654CB00009B/736